ACCLAIM FOR *William Langewiesche*'s

INSIDE THE SKY

"Superb. . . . The man writes with sharpness and wit. He also writes beautifully."
— *Los Angeles Times*

"A thoughtful and absorbing personal account of what a pilot sees, feels and observes as he guides his plane through the skies." — *Parade*

"As a writer, he's a sharp observer and gifted stylist whose sentences . . . often have a kind of poetic precision."
— *The Washington Post Book World*

"Eminently readable. . . . *Inside the Sky* is one of those books you can take to the beach, confident that you'll escape into the mind of a writer who has adventured well."
— *USA Today*

"The prose is beautiful and its chill is difficult to shake off."   —*The Seattle Times*

"The essays in this book deliver . . . a fresh, fearless, and fond view."   —*The Boston Globe*

"His style is spare, powerfully evocative, and infused with the sensibility of one who has seen things from above."
     —*The Atlantic Monthly*

"It's a good book, and I think pilots will enjoy it because, whether he intended to or not, William Langewiesche was as much pilot as poet when writing *Inside the Sky*."   —*Flying*

William Langewiesche

INSIDE THE SKY

William Langewiesche is a correspondent for
The Atlantic Monthly. A professional pilot for
many years, he is the author of *Cutting for Sign*
and *Sahara Unveiled*. He lives in California.

ALSO BY

William Langewiesche

Cutting for Sign

Sahara Unveiled

INSIDE

THE

SKY

William Langewiesche

INSIDE THE SKY

A Meditation on Flight

VINTAGE DEPARTURES

Vintage Books / A Division of Random House, Inc. / New York

FIRST VINTAGE DEPARTURES EDITION, JULY 1999

Copyright © 1998 by William Langewiesche

All rights reserved under International and Pan-American Copyright Conventions. Published in the United States by Vintage Books, a division of Random House, Inc., New York, and simultaneously in Canada by Random House of Canada Limited, Toronto. Originally published in hardcover in the United States by Pantheon Books, a division of Random House, Inc., New York, in 1998.

Vintage Books, Vintage Departures, and colophon are trademarks of Random House, Inc.

Portions of this work have appeared in *The Atlantic Monthly*.

Grateful acknowledgment in made to the following for permission to reprint previously published material: *Warren Faidley:* Excerpt from "In Harm's Way" by Warren Faidley (*Weatherwise*, Washington, D.C., December 1992). Reprinted by permission of Warren Faidley. *University of New Mexico, School of Architecture and Planning:* Excerpts from "The Need of Being Versed in Country Things" (Spring 1951), "The Stranger's Path" (Fall 1957), "The Abstract World of the Hot Rodder" (Winter 1957-58), "Jefferson, Thoreau, and After" (Winter 1965-66), by J. B. Jackson (*Landscape Magazine,* Berkeley, CA). Reprinted by permission of University of New Mexico, School of Architecture and Planning.

The Library of Congress has cataloged the Pantheon Books edition as follows:
Langewiesche, William.
Inside the sky : a meditation on flight / William Langewiesche.
p. cm.
ISBN 0-679-42983-2
1. Langewiesche, William—Anecdotes. 2. Air pilots—United States—Anecdotes. 3. Air travel—Anecdotes. 4. Flight—Anecdotes. I. Title.
TL540.L272A3 1998
629.13'092—dc21 97-49844
CIP

Vintage ISBN: 0-679-75007-X

Author photograph © Robert Lindley

www.vintagebooks.com

Printed in the United States of America
10 9 8 7 6 5

To Jim and Josie Bennington

CONTENTS

1. The View from Above / 3

2. The Stranger's Path / 27

3. The Turn / 56

4. On a Bombay Night / 93

5. Inside an Angry Sky / 114

6. Slam and Jam / 156

7. Valujet 592 / 190

ACKNOWLEDGMENTS

Thanks to Dan Frank, Cullen Murphy, Chuck Verrill, and Bill Whitworth. Thanks also to my family, Minouche, Matthew, and Anna Langewiesche. And thanks finally to those few pilots and interested passengers who have shared with me the inner experience of the sky.

INSIDE

THE

SKY

ONE

The View from Above

AFTER A CENTURY OF FLYING, we still live at a moment of emergence like that experienced by creatures first escaping from the sea. For us the emergence has been given meaning because we can think about it, and can perhaps understand the nature of our liberation. Mechanical wings allow us to fly, but it is with our minds that we make the sky ours. The old measures of distance no longer apply, in part because we hop across the globe in single sittings, but also because in doing so we visit a place which even just above our homes is as exotic and revealing as the most foreign destination. This book is a travel book about that place, and it takes the form of a spiral climb. At the end it will arrive overhead of the point where now it begins, with the idea that flight's greatest gift is to let us look around.

At first I mean a simple form of looking around, and one that requires little instruction—just gazing down at the ordinary scenery sliding by below. The best views are views of familiar things, like cities and farms and bottle-necked freeways. So set aside the beauty of sunsets, the majesty of mountains, the imprint of winds on golden prairies. The world beneath our wings has become a human artifact, our most spontaneous and complex creation. Tourists may not like to contemplate the evidence, with its hints of greed and self-destruction, but the fact remains that the old sterilized landscapes—like designated outlooks and pretty parks and sculpted gardens—have become obsolete, and that it is largely the airplane that has made them so. The aerial view is something entirely new. We need to admit that it flattens the world and mutes it in a rush of air and engines, and that it suppresses beauty. But it also strips the façades from our constructions, and by raising us above the constraints of the treeline and the highway it imposes a brutal honesty on our perceptions. It lets us see ourselves in context, as creatures struggling through life on the face of a planet, not separate from nature, but its most expressive agents. It lets us see that our struggles form patterns on the land, that these patterns repeat to an extent which before we had not known, and that there is a sense to them.

Discovering that sense requires not only that we look outside while flying but that we get over the illusion of smallness, the "Everything looks like a toy!" that blinds us at first to what we see. I write "us" but frankly mean "them" or "you." The truth is I can only imagine learning to see from the air, because my father was a pilot with pilot friends, and I grew up inside their airplanes, gazing at the world below. Day after day through the seasons and years we wandered the sky, and I sat looking outside. To make the time pass I picked points on the airplane—a strut, a rivet, a fairing on the leading edge of a wing—and used those points as sighting devices against the ground to measure the airplane's speed and to define flight's independent paths across the landscape: for a while along a country lane, but then straight across a field and through someone's swimming pool, over a factory, into a city and out again. It was quite early in my childhood, as these unusual paths began effortlessly to fit together, that I developed a pilot's integrated sense of the earth's geometry.

This was in the 1960s, the merest moment after the Wright brothers. When I first flew alone, in a sailplane at the age of fourteen, the experience seemed so normal to me that I have practically no memory of it now. It wasn't until college, when I took an air-taxi job and began carrying passengers for hire, people unaccustomed to flight, that I realized there was anything unusual about the view. Of course, some passengers did not want to look outside. But others were curious. For me it was like witnessing Stone Age people seeing photographs for the first time, getting used to the scale, then turning with growing excitement from the magic to the content of the picture.

These passengers had ridden on the airlines but had been herded into their cabin seats, distracted by magazines, and given shoulder-height triple-pane windows at right angles to the direction of flight. They had been encouraged not to look outside but rather the opposite—to draw the shades for the movie and pretend not to fly at all. And now suddenly they found themselves in a cockpit wrapped in glass, awash in brilliant light, in a small airplane lingering near the ground.

Some passengers simply could not understand the view. I remember a pristine young woman who, ten miles off the San Francisco coast, looked down from our airplane at a ship plowing through the Pacific swells, then looked up at me and smiled prettily.

I was charmed. I said, "What do you think?"

She said, "Is this the Napa Valley?"

The airplane was noisy. I said, "The what?"

She repeated it, less certainly. "The Napa Valley?"

I may have laughed. She looked concerned. Only later did I understand. First flights can confuse the senses and cause normal people to stop thinking.

On another occasion I had a passenger who during a smooth flight at 15,000 feet over Baltimore suspected that perhaps he had died and gone not to heaven but to a strange and suspended place like a purgatory. He meant this quite literally. His face turned numb and chalky white, as if he were about to faint. I asked him what was wrong.

He stammered a confused admission: Had we by chance been in a mid-air collision back there over Wilmington when the controller warned us about that oncoming airplane which we never spotted? The question put me in the unusual position of having to assure someone that both he and I were indeed still alive. These are the things they don't tell you about when you learn to fly.

He was a German art dealer from Berlin and New York, and he did not know Baltimore. The softness of flight had combined with the visible abandonment of the streets below to give him the feeling of death. I explained that it was Super Bowl Sunday and that all Baltimore was watching the game on television. He had been long enough in the United States to understand. The color returned slowly to his skin. I think then that he became interested in the view, which was indeed the view of a sort of afterlife—or of a city still in decline.

The German would have felt better over Berlin or New York not because they are healthier cities but because reading the ground from an airplane is easier if you understand some of the local customs. Residents of Baltimore would see their city from the air more clearly than any transient foreigner, and would find the landscape not dormant or deadly, but compelling. Rather than simply knowing about the Super Bowl, they might share with the city below a genuine interest in the game's outcome—and as result they might not even see a Baltimore in decline. Who could say then whose view was deeper, theirs or mine? But I do know that they would not choose that moment in flight to prefer watching television, because television is dull compared to the view of home from overhead.

I have imagined teaching the aerial view. The best approach would be to apprentice young children as I was apprenticed, to teach them without elaboration simply by flying them to different places, encouraging them to navigate, and to make the translations between maps and the world. Effortlessly they would develop the habit of seeing the world from above, and the more subtle trick while on the ground of understanding the scale and orientation of their surroundings. Flying at its best is a way of thinking. Because of that, once having left the earth's surface, people never again quite return to it. But also because of that, adults often find it hard to make the leap. They simply have spent too many years on the ground. To teach them the aerial view you would have to overcome that landlubbing prejudice which equates driving on a country road, or sleeping in a hotel and visiting the restaurant part of town, with having "been" somewhere, to the exclusion of other possibilities.

I have a friend, a historian at Princeton University, who upon my return from a low-altitude flight up the Eastern seaboard denied that I had actually visited the places I had overflown—the farmed and citied coastal plain from Georgia to New Jersey and in between. I did not invite my friend's judgment, but he offered it anyway, argumentatively, because he could not shake a certain cramped sense of possession that he had acquired while driving the same route the summer before. He was a jealous sort of traveler, like those who return from tours convinced that theirs is the only authentic experience among the natives of some faraway land. Pilots are generally less-educated types, but they are more charitable about geography. In all my time among them, the endless hours sitting in cockpits and waiting around airports, I have never heard one speak small-mindedly of a landscape. Maybe because the aerial view is unrestrained, it can also be generous.

I offered to introduce my friend to it, not by following his road trip from above but by taking him on a shorter flight over Princeton, his hometown, where his sense of possession was justified. He accepted my offer, and on a crisp and sunlit morning was surprised by the density of the university campus, by the alignment of the streets, by the nearness of the New York skyline, by the extent of the new suburban forest. He was interested in the generational growth of office parks, the division of the farms, and the inflated architecture of new houses on small lots like the coming of California to the East. I thought, specialists may measure the increments of change on the ground and may in fact disdain the "naïveté" of the untutored aerial view, but with just one short flight almost anyone can read the outline of the story from up here—in this case, the conclusion of New Jersey's farming life. The aerial view is a democratic view. My friend was interested also in local details like the capricious turns of a certain Hopewell Valley road, and the full extent of a new golf course, and the pattern of old overgrown cow paths converging on a converted barn, and a hidden patch of wilderness by a brook, and the torn shingled roof of another professor's house. Each earned a comment. But he asked me to circle only when we came to his own house, built among others near an expensive day school. He was absorbed, as all people are, by the unexpected proportions and angles and by the strange lay of a familiar neighborhood.

"It's like seeing your face in the mirror for the first time," I suggested.

My friend did not answer. From riding the airlines, he insisted still on the airplane as just a better sort of train, and he was secretly proud of his impatience with the tedium of flight—such impatience being the mark of the modern traveler. In life he had crossed those thresholds of success and self-confidence beyond which he could not easily learn or change his mind. After we landed, he said he remained unconvinced. Of course. And he will not read this book, which is meant as a guide to a still unsettled place in the human experience. But during the flight he did not once turn away from the view of the old settled place, and that was a start.

THE BEST AERIAL VIEWS are low views, but only down to a certain altitude, because there is also such a thing as flying too low to see. This happens at that height above the ground where, depending on the airplane's speed, the scenery rushes by too quickly. From the cockpit of a jet flown at treetop level at, say, 500 miles an hour, the rushing-by is sometimes described in schoolchild terms as a blur. In fact, to the accustomed eye the land remains visually distinct—a complex mix of definable points, of trees and houses and mountaintops. The points slide by in a spectrum of softening speed, from brutally fast directly below, to merely brisk one mile ahead, to not quite stationary up on the distant horizon. There is no blurring to it. You register the points coming in time, and can slow things down by looking a bit farther away.

But if not a blurring, there is indeed a visual frustration to such high-speed treetop flight, and it is a structural one. The details which pass by slowly enough to make sense of are precisely those details which lie too far away to see clearly. For example, you know it's a house that just went by, but for lack of time or clarity you cannot consider its design and setting, or the litter in its back yard—the house as an expression of its inhabitants. The airplane jars through upwelling surface winds. Its speed dominates your thoughts like an obsession. No matter how you twist and turn, you cannot get beyond it.

Even at a relatively slow 200 miles an hour, speed may rob the low view of its content. The obvious solution is to throttle back and fly still more slowly—and that indeed you can do, though not economically in a jet. I will ignore the levitational magic of helicopters, which can hover in any direction, matching the contours of the land, but which are inefficient, disruptive, and nearly as expensive as a jet to operate. For about the cost of driving a car you can fly an old two-seat, propeller-driven airplane and float low across the countryside at road speeds—slow enough to see the hats on the farmers and to judge the quality of their work.

And even that now seems too fast. Let children dream of their supersonic futures. For today's practitioner, the advance is rather at the other end of the scale, with a foot-launched aircraft in which the pilot hangs on shrouds from a wing made of loose fabric like a sail. How appropriate that the French, who are good sailors, have championed this form of aircraft. Calling it the paraglider, they developed it in the 1980s as an alternative to standard delta-wing hang gliders, which are exhilarating to fly, and reasonably safe, but which suffer from the weight and bulk of their tubular frames even when disassembled. The paraglider by contrast has no frame, weighs about the same as a family's picnic lunch, and can be stuffed into a rucksack and carried easily up a mountain. In essence, it is a rectangular high-performance parachute, a close relative to the tethered "parasails" pulled by powerboats at beach resorts, with the important difference that it has no connection to the ground and flies independently, under the pilot's control.

High on some mountain, you invert the fabric on the ground behind you, strap yourself into a seat-harness, and with a tug on the shrouds allow the wind to send the wing aloft directly overhead, where it assumes a cambered form and floats at the ready. With a short run downhill you give it flying speed. It answers by lifting you off your feet, and beginning to coast downhill toward the valley below. Once it gains speed it flattens its glide angle, and takes you out across the trees, the ravines, and the valley itself. The experience is primordial, a feeling of lift and wind like a throwback to the earliest elemental era of flight, before the Wright brothers, when pioneers like the great Berliner Otto Lilienthal floated downhill on homemade wings.

Lilienthal was a mechanical engineer, the manager of a factory that manufactured small steam engines. He crashed and died in 1898, at age forty-eight, after having made 2,000 hang gliding flights, the longest of which lasted fifteen seconds. It seems quaint now that he flew only on weekends and that he fell to his death at walking speed from only fifty feet up—but he was doing serious work, and he knew it. The epitaph on his tombstone records his famous words, *Opfer müssen gebracht werden,* or "Sacrifices must be made." If that now seems like the wrong way to approach the weekend, it was the right way in the 1890s, because at any cost the time had come for human flight.

The difference for us today is not that the designs have improved, though they have, but that as a species we have now had a century of experience inside the sky. The modern paraglider does not advance history but offers the human animal a bit of stitched fabric, some lines, and a harness—a cheap personal portable wing. The flying of such aircraft has become an indulgence and does not call for heroics. In turn, this means that our flying is safer.

There is risk to any flight, of course, and pilots do die in paragliders. They die not because paragliding is unregulated—though in the United States it remains delightfully so—but because of the physics of flight. The slowest and simplest flying machines are particularly vulnerable to the winds and dependent upon the pilot's athletic reactions. Those reactions take a while to develop. Wilbur and Orville Wright, who started as bicycle builders in Dayton, Ohio, set about designing, building, and flying the world's first practical airplanes after reading Lilenthal's obituary in the local newspaper. Their most important insight was that lift alone was not enough—that once in flight the pilot would have to be given absolute control of the wing. They were careful, cerebral men, but also supremely Midwestern and pragmatic. During their early experiments with gliding in 1901, Wilbur wrote, "If you are looking for perfect safety you will do well to sit on a fence and watch the birds, but if you really wish to learn you must mount a machine and become acquainted with its tricks by actual trial."

This remains almost as true today. Despite our accumulated knowledge of the air, the best way to go about paragliding is not to sign up for a class but simply to borrow a wing and run downhill with it. Borrow a helmet, too, and choose a calm day and a shallow slope—but indulge in the risk. In each hand you hold a handle connected by shrouds to the trailing edge of the wing. Those handles function as the glider's only controls. To turn, you pull one or the other, twisting the fabric of the wing to spoil the lift in the direction you want to go. Because the paraglider flies slowly, at bicycle speeds, it requires only a shallow bank to turn quickly. At the end of the flight, as you skim the ground, you pull both handles at once, causing the entire wing to rear up and to slow further until against a light wind you put your feet down and land with a few steps—or instead, as I have, you go about gently crashing.

The slowness of the paraglider is the feature that interests me here, not because it makes for soft landings but because it promises in theory to provide ordinary humans with the most detailed yet of the aerial views. Sometimes I think that people should, after all, take classes in paragliding, but that those classes should be taught at every public high school in the country and offered as alternatives not only to gym but to the tedious courses in "civics" and American geography. This is not a serious proposal, of course, because we have taught ourselves if anything to worship safety—to fasten our seatbelts, to act responsibly, and to follow the reasonable paths through life. *Opfer müssen* nicht *gebracht werden*. Imagine the price to pay each time a student landed badly and was injured or killed. But imagine also the arrival of an entire generation in which people truly had learned to see themselves from above.

Such dreaming aside, paragliders in recent years have encountered a practical problem masked as an advance. Through steady improvements in their design and construction, the gliding performance of these sky-sails keeps getting better, and is now nearly fifteen to one, which means they can fly fifteen feet forward for every foot they descend. This does not approach the sixty-to-one ratios of enclosed sailplanes, but it is about that of delta-wing hang gliders. Accompanying the flattened glide angle is a lessening of sink rates to about 200 feet per minute. The numbers are important because they are more than matched by the vertical fluctuations of ordinary winds. As a result, paraglider pilots can now soar, which means they can ride updrafts, gain altitude, stay aloft for hours, and even fly trips of a hundred miles and more. My own small regret is that these possibilities encourage a record-setting mentality in which flying becomes a "sport" turned in on itself and pilots come to consider the landscape only for the chances it creates—the coastal ridge, the sun-heated parking lot, the swirl of dust that marks the start of rising air. To soar you have to stay high and exploit every opportunity. The ground becomes the enemy. You can't afford to see it in detail.

One answer is to abandon soaring and strap an engine to your back, and this indeed is now done. Again the French have led the way. They call the result the powered paraglider and have established enough of a following to support two stores in Paris alone. The wing is slightly shorter. The engine is mounted on a backframe and drives a four-bladed pusher-propeller in a wire cage—an arrangement, including fuel and a small battery for in-flight electrical starts, which weighs about thirty pounds, and which the pilot wears in addition to the standard wing harness. This time along with the control handles, you hold a throttle lever connected by cable to the engine. You take off downhill or on level ground after a short run into the wind with the engine roaring. For the outside observer it is a peculiar sight: this two-legged animal with a parachute overhead and noisy machinery strapped to his back, running awkwardly across a field, then retracting his legs and flying. It is peculiar for the pilot too, until your wings take hold and pull you into the sky. Then suddenly it feels quite natural. The powered paraglider may be the most primitive airplane that has ever existed, but it offers a genuine form of flight. You can climb in it one mile high and hover there for hours.

Better yet you can pack it into an airliner, then unpack it somewhere new and fly it low. I have a Parisian friend named François Lagarde, a pioneer of this technique, who has flown his powered paraglider across Tunisia, Niger, Cameroon, Martinique, and Thailand. Even the most timid traditionalists would have to admit that thereby he has "visited" those places. Other than making occasional adjustments to the wing, he has little to do in flight but to look around. Lagarde flies low, sometimes below the treetops, following footprints and trails, chasing rabbits. He maneuvers among giraffes and elephants and smells the dry dung and wet earth, the grasses, trees, and flowers. He waves to villagers and alights like a bird in those villages where people wave back. He flies in the United States and France as well, and he talks of China next. All this may seem like another exercise in European adventurism, but Lagarde is not a faddist. There are good reasons for his obsession. He is extroverted and social and unafraid, and he wants to experience the world in its full vitality. He knows that the view from above is frank and unobstructed. And he has learned that the very low view, when it is also very slow, is often also intimate.

BUT HE AND I have different goals in flight. Although my writing now takes me to far-off places in the world, as a pilot I am still most interested in the view of the place I know best, which is this country here. And although I understand the interest of the slowest European flight and admire the education that sustains it, I am an American pilot with an American taste for waste, a nervous hunger for speed and power only half justified by the size of the continent. It is true that I would rather fly my own propeller airplane where I choose to go than fly someone else's jet much faster where others choose to send me. But I won't pretend that I always cherish the view.

I have even used speed maliciously to blind my passengers. For several years I worked as an air-taxi pilot along the Mexican border of west Texas. It was a wild part of the world, infested with smugglers of drugs and guns, and potentially dangerous for any public for-hire pilot. I knew it when I moved there, and I was determined to stay out of trouble. When one evening a rancher from the Rio Grande offered me six months' earnings to "repossess" an airplane in Mexico and fly it low into the United States, I easily said no. The rancher was feeling me out; it was clear that the repossessed airplane would be loaded with dope. But I was hungry, and I did take some of the more ambiguous flights that an older pilot might have declined.

I flew small single-pilot airplanes. The danger for me, as for ordinary taxi drivers, was bad neighborhoods and aggressive passengers. The threat came not from the big drug cartels but from random free-lance operators who could cross the Rio Grande from Mexico with a small load of cocaine and, once having arrived in the unpoliceable no-man's land along the U.S. side of the river, call for an air taxi to fly in and pick them up, then turn around and fly them north, far beyond the border defenses. We were a local flying service with frequent and legitimate flights to the Rio Grande, which made us the perfect target for such a scheme. As a pilot, it was of little help not to know the contents of the luggage. You could be convicted of smuggling nonetheless, and even without going to prison you could lose your right to fly, which for a pilot is nearly the same. Worse yet, a high-strung passenger could, upon arrival at a lonely landing strip, simply decide to silence you. It was a real possibility. The ghosts of murdered pilots haunt isolated runways all through the Southwest.

I thought I could control the danger by bringing along a strong friend—a 250-pound Chicano named Tweeter who worked as a mechanic at the airport and who played the copilot, glowering beside me in the cockpit with his drooping mustache and his wrapped sunglasses, armed with a fire extinguisher and a baseball bat, hoping for trouble. The worst flights announced themselves beforehand by phone: a harried stranger on the river, wanting immediate service for no clear reason, forgetting to question the cost. I want to think that we never carried narcotics, though in truth I do not know. I did fly through troubled currents, and because of Tweeter I flew through them without fear.

But once when he was not at the airport I got a suspicious call for a pickup at a remote runway on the border, and I had to decide whether to set off for the Rio Grande alone. The caller was a woman, a stranger who spoke with the flat nasal vowels of the Midwest. She said her husband was sick and needed to get to Odessa, an oil town up north on the interstate. I took a minute to scribble a few calculations of time and fuel. She understood my silence as reluctance.

"Just hold on," she said, and she muffled the phone with her hand. Then she said, "He says we pay cash—dollars." She was used to following her husband's lead.

I gave her an estimate of the cost. I said, "It's a standard rate, by the hour, the return trip too."

"Who's the pilot? Are you the pilot?"

"Yes."

"He says just get down here fast."

If the man was that sick, why didn't he go to a doctor there? The call was all wrong. The woman's urgency worried me—it sounded like panic. But I started the airplane anyway and taxied and took off, because I needed the work.

It was a summer afternoon, with clouds building over the jagged west Texas peaks and a dust plume rising from a cattle truck moving down a dry dirt road. My destination was the runway outside of Presidio, the last town in the United States, and the hottest. The route led south across a grassland basin divided by barbed wire into vast pastures, some cropped close by cattle to the color of dirt, others more luxuriant and yet still brown. Isolated ranch houses huddled with sheds under cottonwood trees. I had once loved that landscape self-indulgently, for the purity and beauty of its wide open space, and for its comforting diminution of my own existence—the scale it gave to my worries and ambitions and the reminder it offered me that these concerns mattered less than I tended to believe. Such was the appeal of the wilderness to me—something I no longer feel, the appeal of a surrender. But I was learning a new way of seeing the landscape now, which was more acute in its acknowledgment of the human presence there and of my own involvement. Flight forced this on me. The enormity and emptiness of the place suggested no longer its virgin splendor but rather its human history—from the first tentative routes along the dry creeks, to the assertive overlay of the transcontinental railroad, to the birth and now death of the small towns.

Despite their beauty, the ranches were dying, too. Evidence lay not only in the decay of the old buildings, some recently abandoned, but also in the blossoming of flamboyant new estates. The estates were built by rich outsiders who made their money elsewhere and cared more about the esthetic of the land than about its productivity. I thought this was probably a good thing, since there was little risk of subdivision here, and land once wrested from the grasp of authentic ranching did seem to return to a deeper state of grace. Preservation, too, is part of the human landscape.

But it was the international boundary that occupied me today—a trace on a map, a dirty little river where two unequal neighbors met, an artificial and dangerous and unfair and necessary line. The river glinted at the bottom of a deep geological rift. I came at it from the side, crossing the rift's mountainous lip and descending steeply. The grassland soon succumbed to the desert, nature's equalizer, so that along the river, by narrow scenic standards, both sides of the border looked about the same.

The narrowness of the view is a problem particular to the ground. Few tourists ever went to Presidio, but those who did often got the astonishing impression that the border there hardly existed. Residents, too, because they freely forded the river, could share that illusion. But from the air the view always widens. Forget the revelations of a shared humanity that astronauts are told to talk about. Such revelations are pitched to placate the opponents of rocket ships and their budgets. The astronauts simply fly too high to see. What the ordinary aerial view really shows is exactly the opposite of a unified world. Beyond wind and water, it is human history that now sculpts the earth.

In flight you could never have mistaken the Rio Grande for just a river. With the exception of tiny Presidio and its satellite settlements, the U.S. side had been abandoned on private as well as public lands to the preservation of a new wilderness. Mexico by comparison made no excuses for its humanity. Big tough Ojinaga spread its dirty streets over the hills and extended a network of rutted roads to fifty miles of river villages—a band of hardscrabble civilization fastened tightly to the Texan underbelly. Somewhere below, a highway sign mentioned 500-year-old fields, but there was little real farming left. The border people got by as border people do, by smuggling. A few smugglers became rich and built big houses in fortified compounds, but most people merely survived. They let their churches and villages fall into ruin. And this, too, was obvious from the air.

The Presidio International Airport had a single sloping runway just off the highway. It was called "international" because it also had an outside pay phone from which, if you flew in from Mexico, you could in principle call on Customs to come up from the river for the entry formalities. This happened maybe twice a year. Presidio was probably the quietest international airport in the United States.

Mine was the only airplane there that afternoon. I shut it down in the sun beside a wrecked trailer in which for a while a missionary pilot had lived while proselytizing the river people. He had told me he was a soldier in the army of the Lord. After only a half-year he had retreated, leaving the trailer with broken windows to collect the desert air.

The sun lay low. My passengers came from the trailer's shadow and hobbled hurriedly toward the airplane holding each other in an awkward embrace, carrying a half-empty gym bag. The woman was tall and bony and wore her jeans too tight; her husband was taller, and muscular, but walked hunched over, so that his hair fell forward in greasy strands across his face. His clothes were filthy, as if he had rolled in the dirt. He stumbled, and the woman held him up. They pushed into the airplane without a word and sprawled onto the back seats.

I said, "Wait a minute."

The woman snapped, "Just get us out of here!"

"I want to know what's the matter with him."

"He got a bug in Mexico."

But his face was bruised, and his eyes were strange, both furtive and aggressive. I figured that he had been beaten and that he was drugged, maybe against his will. He glared at me and mumbled something I could not make out. The woman draped her arm across his chest, pushing him gently against the seat. She touched her head to his and murmured soothingly into his ear. This seemed not to work.

"What's in the bag?" I asked.

"Sneakers and a T-shirt."

"I'd like to see."

She handed me the bag grudgingly. "There's a gun, too, but it's safe, so go ahead and check it."

It was a 9mm pistol. I dropped the clip, checked the chamber, zipped the gun into the bag, and put the bag up front beside me.

The man said, "He's a bitch."

The woman didn't care. She wanted to get away from the border. She gentled the man back into his seat again.

An admonition in the language of a commandant is often posted at airports: "Maintain thine airspeed, lest the earth rise up and smite thee." In straight English, something similar should be said about landscapes as well. With these two frantic people the border—with all its lurking menace, its incipient violence—had reached for me and laid claim to my involvement. I had become a local character, and it did not occur to me to refuse the flight.

Nonetheless I was angry about it, worried not about

contraband or a violent end at the airport in Odessa, but about the threatening attitude of the man in the back seat, and his apparent unpredictability. If from a distance now it seems obvious that the danger lay mostly in my mind, at the time the situation was less clear. Various possibilities arose—that the man could lose his temper and attack me in flight, that either he or she was a pilot and could take over, that partway to Odessa they might put a second gun to my head and force me to some remote runway where they could pull the trigger. I did not know who these people were or how their deal had gone bad, but I sensed they were dangerous to me, and without Tweeter there to protect me I instinctively took the offensive.

After lifting off from the runway at Presidio, I leveled the airplane at fencepost height, so low that we were flying down *inside* the scenery, where the slightest distraction would drive us into the ground. It was a rough ride. For 200 miles I kept us there, without explanation, a short throw from oblivion. It was an act of self-defense but also, I admit, of aggression. These people had menaced me, and here in the air I could reciprocate. The landscape was my ally because I often flew it low when I was alone and I knew every rocky point and power line along the way. Now I could wield it like a weapon and assault my passengers with the airplane's speed. I gambled that even if they were pilots they would not dare to grab the controls or try to resist me. And indeed they did not, but submitted to the landscape's punishment, clutched together on the back seats in their habitual beleaguered embrace. They were strangers to the aerial view—I saw that, and did not relent. Who knows what confusion passed before their eyes. After we landed in Odessa they shoved cash into my hands and fled without waiting for change. I flew home low, too, for the simple thrill of my escape.

I still enjoy the escape of low flight and sometimes go out into the desert to chase at head height along dirt roads, banking vertically to make the turns, pulling up to keep the wingtips from dragging. But it is the richness of the genuine aerial view, something both higher and slower, that I keep returning to. I realize now that the aerial view has formed me, and that I have carried it with me from the cockpit to my more recent work of wandering and writing and reporting about the world. And it is odd how even on the ground, weeks from any airplane, the aerial view seems still to fit. It carries with it the possibility of genuinely free movement, and allows just the right amount of participation with the landscape—neither as distant as an old-fashioned vista nor as entrapping as a permanent involvement.

The Stranger's Path

IT IS STRANGE that the greatest explorer of the aerial
view, the late essayist John Brinkerhoff Jackson, was not a
pilot and indeed rarely flew. I mean "aerial view" now in a
large sense, not just the view from an airplane in flight, but
the habit that it breeds—a frank and distant way of seeing
one's surroundings even when on the ground. Jackson nur-
tured that habit and succeeded with it, only to fail at the
end when in his loneliness he tried to close the uncloseable
distance, to become a part of those surroundings. But even
that failure was an expression of the aerial view.

I can be more specific. Jackson died in 1996, at the age
of eighty-seven, in La Cienega, New Mexico, a working-
class settlement of Spanish-speakers south of Santa Fe
where he had lived for nearly forty years. He never mar-

ried or had children, and he left his considerable fortune to charity. To his neighbors he was known simply as John, a patron of the community, yes, but also a profane and wizened old man who dressed in motorcycle leather, wore tattoos on his arms, and for unknowable reasons chose to work as a janitor and yardman, driving around in a battered pickup truck with rakes and brooms and shovels and a dog named Reesy. To the larger world he was known as J. B. Jackson, the founder in 1951 of *Landscape,* a small magazine not about gardening, as people naturally assume, but about the human geography of America.

Jackson published *Landscape* for seventeen years, until he grew tired of the struggle and sold it for a dollar in 1968. The magazine never ran ads, or turned a profit, or expanded beyond about 3,000 subscribers, but it served as a forum for well-known thinkers about the American scene—a group of social scientists, designers, city planners, and intellectuals for whom the obscurity of the magazine was an attraction. More important, the magazine served as a forum for Jackson himself, a man of profoundly humanistic impulses, who insisted on the worth of ordinary people, and on the value of the spontaneous disorder in what he called the "vernacular" landscape.

The word requires explanation. Jackson borrowed it from its normal usage, where of course it means the native form of ordinary language, as opposed to the literary or learned forms. He reapplied it with a similar meaning to the physical world of cities and inhabited countryside— the commercial strips and unpretentious neighborhoods where most Americans live. "Vernacular" for Jackson meant the everyday evidence of people's ordinary lives, the way they *really* live them, as opposed to the way they are told they should. His admiration for spontaneity was a celebration of humankind, a rebellion against the elitism of designers, and an expression of an anti-authoritarianism which seems to have been his only true political impulse. He was driven to it by his demon, the self-doubt born of a privileged childhood and inherited wealth. But it was also forced on him from the outside, as it is forced on us all by now, by the relentless and encompassing clarity of the aerial view. The connection to the "vernacular" is easy to make. Because the aerial view is accepting, it gives fair weight to all the ugliness of society's energetic clutter, the chaotic scarring which spreads across the horizons, and which for anyone but the most close-minded romantic becomes more interesting than a planned or preserved landscape. Jackson claimed to have discovered the view as a boy during the occasional biplane ride when the world sprawled below him like a revelation. Later he made it his life's view because it matched him almost perfectly—aristocratic as any overview must be, but also accessible, democratic, and free.

In the end there were reasons both to admire and to distrust his reactions. He seemed to feel that he had to make a choice, that having recognized the importance of vernacular expression in the landscape, he had to embrace it as well. This eventually brought him into conflict with the rising naturalist movement, which contained more powerful voices than his. While they talked about the importance of unspoiled nature, Jackson kept insisting on the value of the casual human touch. And though in principle he was right and they were wrong, in political practice it worked the other way around. He became by inference an apologist for greed, overzealous construction, and the gratuitous consumption of the earth's resources.

His background was partly to blame; as a well-bred gentleman he hated to quarrel. Still, after quitting the magazine he continued to speak his mind, for ten years as a part-time lecturer at Harvard and Berkeley, and then back home at La Cienega, where every evening, after days spent cleaning yards and gas stations, he continued to write about the importance of understanding his everyday surroundings. His work was collected into six books, one of which, *A Sense of Place, a Sense of Time,* won the award for essays in 1995 from PEN, the professional writers' association. That was another side of Jackson. He brought to his pages the sensibilities of a lyricist and the endurance of an unencumbered man.

But for me Jackson's significance was more direct. Here at last was someone who, despite his obvious failings, made the case for looking at the world as one naturally does from the air, with clarity and sympathy, and yet with that certain detachment which precludes the urge for immediate intervention. It is curious that he never exploited the tool that best suited him, the airplane, because he certainly did understand its power. In his magazine's inaugural issue, in the spring of 1951, he wrote:

It is from the air that the true relationship between the natural and the human landscape is first clearly revealed. The peaks and canyons lose much of their impressiveness when seen from above; their vertical dimensions are scarcely discernible except for the blue shadows they cast; and the non-human portion of the country becomes an almost featureless tawny brown surface. What catches our eye and arouses our interest is not the sandy washes and the naked rocks, but the evidences of man: the lonely windmills and tanks with trails converging upon them; the long straight lines of fences, often dividing the overgrazed range from the one properly managed; the broad pattern of contour plowing and tractor cultivating. The farmhouses appear to be surrounded by a grove of trees and a complexity of gardens and corrals and yards. The roads meander to the nearest village or railroad, or to the highway and the city. The harmonious and intricate design which man makes in the course of living and working on the face of the earth slowly evolves beneath us; bright green, dark brown, white, or glittering in the sun, silent and empty of movement (so it appears) except for the small shadow of the plane rippling over fields and roofs. It is a picture we are seeing, an image which stirs us not only because of its beauty and vastness but because of its meaning.

No one who has experienced this spectacle . . . can have failed to be fascinated by it, nor to wonder at the variety of men's ways of coming to terms with nature. Why are some stretches of land thickly settled with villages almost within sight of one another, while others are occupied by great rectangular fields and a few lonely houses? What brought into being so close a network of roads and trails and bridges? Some farmhouses are small and primitive, others have a dozen satellite buildings; and some are so close to their neighbors as to form villages and small towns. And how to account for the many types among the towns themselves?

Jackson was a sophisticate, though later at La Cienega he pretended not to be, and he knew from the start that simple answers would never suffice. He wrote:

The asking of such questions is more important than the finding of an answer. It means that like the air traveler, we have acquired a new and valuable perspective on the world of men, and with it eventually comes the realization there is really no such thing as a dull landscape or farm or town. Countrysides can be poor or sickly, or the prey of one serious ailment— drought or revolution or the collapse of a market— and it is well for us to know the symptoms. But none is without character, no habitat of man is without the appeal of the existence which originally created it.

He concluded the essay with an apparently simple proposition that for the following forty-five years would dog his work: "A rich and beautiful book is always open before us. We have but to learn to read it."

The "book" of course is the landscape, whether viewed from above or from within. When Jackson read it, often from the saddle of his cherished BMW motorcycle, he discovered a symbolic terrain dense with hidden meaning. For me, the ordinary pilot, he was most revealing on the subject of the great American grid, the rectangular survey lines with which for a century after 1785 we transformed our still-unlimited space and with which we ordered and anticipated the growing nation south and west of the Appalachians. Though we have in important ways moved beyond it, the grid remains the context of much of North America life—a radical and pervasive tableau within which we are born and struggle and die, and across which now we fly.

North, south, east, and west run the lines. A fence, a farm road, a row of trees, the tight streets of a sleepy county seat, a uniquely American graffiti. Only in the sky can we emerge from these surroundings to discover the scale of the experiment that has been worked upon us. Looking outside while in flight we can find winding suburbs, and islands of preserved wilderness, and still-defiant deserts, but we would never mistake this country for an older or smaller world.

Jackson recognized the problems with the grid: its disregard of the terrain's natural contours, and of watersheds, and of the needs of dry-grass ranching; its reduction of land to a mere commodity, a property to be used up and discarded, or to be too readily exchanged for cash; its sheer crushing monotony. He warned against idealizing the past and lapsing into what he called "sentimental antiquarianism," and he was of course aware of what happened to the Indians who resisted the grid or got in its way. Nonetheless, he thought it important to remember the grid's utopian origins—not just the carving up of the frontier, but the creation of an egalitarian society of small towns and citizen farmers holding equal and interchangeable units of land, a Jeffersonian model in which urban suffering and the bad weight of central government might be counterbalanced by a vast and enlightened countryside.

The survey was one of history's most ambitious political acts, and it is all the more remarkable because by modern standards it was carried out in the blind, on the basis of uncertain maps and crudely measured lines. Only today, because of the airplane, is it possible actually to *see* the continental extent of the effort. There below our wings lies the evidence of who we are, and where our nation has come from, an important artifact of the American experience. The grid is not uniform. Along the Mississippi River and in the Southwest it accommodates the original French and Spanish patterns, and everywhere it shows evidence of change, not only the consolidation of properties and the slow abandonment of the agrarian democratic ideal, but more significantly still, the overlay of an entirely different national pattern based on movement and speed: the contour-hugging railroads, the railroad towns, and the highways and cloverleafs and car cities that followed.

Jackson believed in the need not only to face such changes but to understand and appreciate the relationship of ordinary people to them. He was a radical, and believed in letting downtowns die. He was a historian but also an anti-preservationist. He wrote, "The towns and small cities of Europe are fast being submerged by a flood of good taste; theirs is the fixed smile of welcome to tourists; over here we still retain a varied and exuberant beauty."

Exuberant and ever changing. Over just the past decade an entirely new American landscape has begun to take form. Based on the microprocessor, it lies beyond the pattern of roads in a terrain of shifting workplaces and late-night hours and communities of the mind. Where it lies in the cities it remains largely invisible, hidden among the low-slung office buildings and subdivisions of the urban sprawl, most noticeable perhaps for its very nothingness. But it has also spawned a change in the countryside, which here and there is visible from the air—a pattern of incongruously sophisticated houses, often with pool and private playground, dispersed like one-family missions into the distant mountains and forests far from any commute, a speckling of modernity. There are people in Colorado on California time, and people in California on New York time, and slowly they are forming the landscape to fit themselves.

Jackson seemed to anticipate such possibilities as early as 1965:

> It is of no use trying to resurrect the vanished forms, beautiful though they may have been; their philosophical justification has gone. All we can do is to produce landscapes for unpredictable men, where the free and democratic intercourse of the Jeffersonian landscape can somehow be combined with the intense self-awareness of the solitary romantic. The

existential landscape, without absolutes, without pro-
totypes, devoted to change and mobility and the free
confrontation of men, is already taking form around
us. It has vitality, but it is neither physically beautiful
nor socially just. Our American past has an invaluable
lesson to teach us: a coherent, workable landscape
evolves where there is a coherent definition not of
man but of man's relation to the world and to his fellow men.

And who could disagree? This was Jackson in high
style—an uninhibited intellect breaking free of the ground
and looping through the thin air of abstraction. His work
was flamboyant, incautious, and fiercely sincere. It was
up to academic geographers to follow behind, doing the
drudge work, digging up the details about specific landscapes—the cautious measurements and footnoted his-
tories to be filed away in university libraries for future
reference. Little wonder that many mainstream academics
remained wary of Jackson. He claimed to respect them,
but he clearly had no desire to participate in their incre-
mental approach to collective knowledge. As a young man
he had studied history at Harvard and architecture at MIT,
but he had earned no advanced degrees. Yes, he was well
educated in a classical way, and he spoke good French and
German, and he had traveled, but the suspicion existed
that he was a dilettante, a rich man using an inherited fortune to purchase legitimacy, free of the discipline imposed
by peer review and academic infighting, or the simple
need to make a living. Some of his assertions were based

on intuition rather than on specific knowledge; and many
of his conclusions were openly speculative. He was always
a humble man, careful to downplay his contribution. But
although he was obviously also a brilliant man, it was fair
to question the nature of his talent, and whether indeed it
was more purely literary than useful or profound. Not
once did he perform the hard and detailed work necessary
to explain in concrete terms the "how" and the "why" of
a specific landscape. His insistence on the importance of
the vernacular was a nice slap at the intellectual elites, but
he himself seemed to refuse to get his hands dirty until he
walked away from his teaching positions and returned full-
time to La Cienega. There, he set about quite literally getting his hands dirty, which is a different thing.

But this is not hard. Jackson was a writer and always only
that. In the years leading up to World War II, he wrote as
a wanderer of the world, with essays, short stories, and a
novel about the rise of Nazism in Germany. Later, when
he began to write about the landscape, he came up against
the great limitation of such writing—that in order fully to
explain a landscape, you have to enter so tediously into its
details that readers simply will not follow. Jackson never
got around this limitation. It is possible that he was indeed
lazy and never able to overcome the handicap of his life-
time of privilege, but more likely he sensed as a writer that
his readers were right. If the professors' job was to record
the details anyway (and to read them), Jackson's job was
closer to my own—to suggest quietly that no special education is needed, and no extra time, and that we draw from

the landscape what we bring to it once we remember to look around. Jackson's admiration for the vernacular was a necessary part of the approach. In order to decipher his world, he had to start by embracing it. It is probably obvious that the same is true for us in the air. We can draw nothing from the view if we turn away from it in distaste or slide shut the cabin shades to look at pictures of prettier things.

It is also probably obvious that such an approach is a matter of personality. Jackson was in his early thirties when World War II came along, and he enlisted in the Army in a fit of patriotism, or ennui, and was sent as a common soldier to the ugly border town of El Paso, Texas, where to his surprise he discovered what he had been missing—the physical challenges, the discipline, and especially the easy companionship of ordinary Americans turned soldiers. The simple life did not last long. Because of Jackson's credentials, the Army plucked him from the barracks, made him an intelligence officer, and assigned him to a headquarters staff to campaign across North Africa and Europe. He enjoyed that work, too, and he later said that its requirements—the map reading and the practical need to know what lay ahead—were what alerted him to the importance and complexity of landscape. It was hardly a new thought. When Jackson consulted the trusty old Baedeker guidebooks for information on the countryside ahead, he was using the same source that the German General Nikolaus von Falkenhorst had turned to a few years before to plan (on Hitler's insane orders, within five hours) the conquest of Norway. Whether ultimately for good or evil, all armies must understand the opposing terrain.

But Jackson began to think about his own terrain as well. Each day when he left the headquarters to gather information on the front lines, he found there the same common soldiers he had known in El Paso, and he was struck by the fullness of the topography that they had created—a shifting landscape of war, rich in symbolism, a place never far from the Germans and yet as immediately American as the high plains of Kansas. Jackson later wrote about this discovery only in tangential terms, as if he never quite seized its practical meaning—that the soldiers did not die for God or government but for something that was more truly theirs. It was a fundamental insight into the experience of battle. Jackson was shot and wounded, and after his recovery he gladly kept fighting. He pretended for a while not to have changed, and after the German collapse he even wrote some traditional guidebooks for the American occupiers, but the truth was he no longer cared that his once cherished European landscapes had been overrun.

Those were the terms of Jackson's rebellion. When he came home from the battlefields he continued to find beauty and grace in the rawness of the human condition. During his final years it became obvious that he had been driven by an emotional need, too—an unfulfilled yearning that must have come before the landscape of war and must in some way have led him to his discoveries there. Where others saw only a torn and brutal terrain, Jackson found an authentic America from which he had been excluded by his upbringing and education. During the war he had for a few years a real reason to participate in it. The horror that he encountered came decades later, with the slow realization that try as he might to crawl clear of his own background—by simplifying his language and clothes, and ultimately his work—he would never again be able to escape from himself. His frustration surfaced in his writing, in its melancholic tone and insistent modesty, in its stubborn idealization of ordinary Americans, in its attempt to validate their lives, in its implicit recognition that they did not need or value the validation. But he remained disciplined to the end, like an ideal soldier, and never admitted the full extent of his loneliness. He was a humanist condemned to a headquarters life.

Some of his friends doubted the authenticity of his dilemma because they knew that Jackson was never crazy, and they were bewildered by the choices that he made. Edward Hall, an anthropologist who wrote for *Landscape,* told me with a hint of impatience that Jackson would have been a good spymaster. He said there was a separate man within him, peering out without emotion, coldly orchestrating the contradictions of the Jackson persona. This surprised me because Hall was a pilot and had taken Jackson flying and of all people should have understood the ephemeral and isolating qualities of his view.

I guessed that Hall was mistaken about Jackson but that he had picked up on one important part of the story: Jack-

son had developed so powerful a habit of observation that
he was able always to see himself, and must have understood even during his worst moments that his burden of
solitude was also his strength. In that sense, too, Jackson's
view was like a pilot's. Flying alone on stormy nights
among the clouds, I have glimpsed the lights of rain-
slicked villages far below, and I have yearned for ordinary
human company, while at the same time silently exulting
in the extremes of my solitude. Jackson would have understood. And he would have understood as well when I write
that it is possible while flying through a storm to draw survival from the wish for still worse weather and, if that
weather comes, from the grim determination to fight it
out alone.

So allow me this digression. Jackson's life passed like a
long solo flight through the isolation of the sky. He was
engaged to be married during the war, but when he
returned he found that his fiancée had married someone
else. Afterward it appears that he had no other woman, and
no man either for that matter. His father died early. He
loved his mother and cared for her until she died, too. He
had a half-brother on the East Coast, and that brother had
children, and Jackson let himself drift apart from them.
He had his academic acquaintances and the women who
helped him to produce *Landscape,* but those were necessary
professional relationships, office obligations, and they went
no further. In the 1950s he turned his back on the cocktail
circuit of Santa Fe, where people stupidly assumed Jackson
was one of them, and called him "Brink," and after forty

years professed still not to understand his hostility. At home in La Cienega afterward he had new working-class companions, but he kept them at a distance as well, maybe because they in turn could not quite accept him as their equal and friend. Still, he remained a determined humanist. Whether his topic was the meaning of the garage or the dangers of "one-worldism," the underlying subject never changed; in his own distant way he wrote until the end about people.

I never met him, but after his death I flew one winter day to Santa Fe and drove south a few miles through the snowy creek-cut desert to La Cienega. Jackson's house was a big but unassuming adobe structure standing among cottonwood trees, down a sloping dirt driveway below the level of a county road, and so mostly invisible until you were too close quite to see it. It was, I thought, an appropriate setting for the man. He had designed the house and had hired the local farmers and workmen to build it for him, and they had written their names into the concrete floor of the verandah and had returned at least once a year with their children and grandchildren for the banquet that Jackson held every summer for all of La Cienega. But now the house was locked, silent, and not quite empty, as if the life had suddenly been sucked out of it, which it had.

I read the names on the verandah floor, then walked around the outside walls, sloshing in mud and snow to peer through the windows into the big, rough, ranch-style kitchen with its 1950s cabinets and linoleum countertops; into the library with its high wood-beamed ceiling and its bookcase walls; into the bedrooms and the old bathrooms with the old fixtures in need of repair; into a living room wing sealed off from the rest of the house with blankets still nailed over the doors to keep heating costs down.

Jackson had lived frugally. Quiet though it was, the house still reflected his presence. The worn doorways, the scuff marks on the walls, the familiar stains, the cracked tiles—together they constituted the landscape of a single life, sights so familiar that even Jackson, with his habit of observation, must hardly have noticed them. I looked up at the knurled beams of the library ceiling and wondered how often he had studied their patterns with other thoughts in mind. He had written in longhand on sheets of white paper, nights spent alone smoking unfiltered Camels, forming words by the yellow light of electric bulbs. His neighbors in La Cienega knew that he wrote every night, but they did not know about what, and they did not care. After his death, many were surprised to hear of his small fame.

Now the house would be sold, probably to strangers who would know and care less. Hadn't some crazy old man owned the house before? While cleaning up, maybe they would find one of the calling cards that Jackson had printed up after his return from teaching. The cards said "John" and showed the figure of a man with a ladder. Jackson used them to drum up business for what he called the "dog shit detail," his chosen day job. He explained the choice to no one. When an old acquaintance in Santa Fe asked him about it, he grew angry and answered, "I'll tell you what's important—geography!" For a while he pumped gas out at the Texaco, where the commuters saw him as an annoyance, a down-and-out old man who was getting in their way. Once he complained about it to a fellow worker:

"Alfonso, these people run by me like I'm not even here."

"That's the way life is, John."

"Yeah, I guess so, Alfonso."

When Alfonso told me this, he still did not know that Jackson had spent his life observing just that process, or that he had welcomed it. Jackson's house would now be sold, and the new owners would destroy Jackson's traces, and Jackson would have welcomed that as well. He worked, he said, in order to stay alive. But he was the servant of the aerial view, the last person who would have argued for his own special preservation.

JACKSON'S BELOVED LA CIENEGA was a sprawl of subsistence farms and adobe and cinderblock houses scattered for several miles among the cottonwood trees and scrub pines along a dry creek. It had a small community center in a metal building, but no park or playground or store. Jackson lay buried nearby in an unmarked grave in the spare little cemetery by the spare little church.

I found the grave by the remnants of flowers laid upon it, and for a while I just stood there, looking around. It was late in the day, and the sun was going down, coloring the mountain clouds, and the wind had turned cold and was rustling the bare branches of the trees. A guard light switched on, casting a halo through the wood smoke in the air. There were lights also in the few houses I could see, which with their woodpiles and broken-down cars looked rural and poor. A dog barked from the yard of a trailer, and from across the way another dog answered. A pickup truck came down the road, thunked over the bridge, and turned up the dirt track past the community center to the church.

A workman got out, opened the church's doors, and began to rummage around in the back of the truck, pretending not to notice me. After a few minutes I strolled over to ask if I could look inside the church. It was no problem, of course. The workman wore bulky clothes and had a craggy, weathered face as if he had spent most of his life outside in the wind; he told me he had come to fix a hinge on the church door. I asked him if he had known Jackson.

"Everyone knew him," he said. "He wanted us to call him John. He had a funny thing going you know. He'd drive around in that old truck of his doing yard work and cleaning up, and then he'd turn around and hire people here for his own place."

"Why do you think he did that?"

The workman seemed to resent my question. He shrugged as if to say, "Why does it matter to you?" I could not answer what I suspected—that Jackson toward the end had lived like some mythical pilot trapped in flight and unable to land. So I said nothing, and the workman and I looked away from each other for a while. Eventually he spoke again. "You know what John said to me one day? He said he was a lot happier now than when he was a professor."

I said I was not surprised. But I was not convinced either. I wandered through the church, with its whitewashed walls and simple crucifix and its rows of stiff little pews. The priest, I had heard, was a dynamic Panamanian whose main parish was up in Santa Fe. He was known as the Salsa Padre because he was a musician, too, and one night a week he performed and sang at a bar in a local salsa band. He had conducted Jackson's funeral, presiding over a rare mixing of Santa Fe society, in which the Anglo elites stood for an hour shoulder to shoulder with the working-class Spaniards of La Cienega.

Most of the Anglos left before the burial ceremony. One of them, a lady who spoke through clenched teeth, later said to me, "The Spanish went off and did whatever the Spanish do. The Spanish down there, they are a primitive people, you know, and Brink was the *patron* of that wretched little village. It was central to his life, and you can skip the whole thing. It is utterly inexplicable."

But I did not think so. At the church now, I drifted back to the workman, who was tinkering with the door. I asked gently about Jackson's religion.

The man kept working. He said, "Oh yeah, toward the end there he used to bow his head down pretty much."

I thanked him and walked outside to my car. The man

came to the doorway and stood outlined against the bright church light. He must have wondered who I was. Before I got into the car, I waved good-bye. He did not wave back but remained standing there, watching. But he remembered something else that he wanted to say, and he called out, "But God could he cuss, too! I never heard anyone who could cuss like John could!"

In the morning I found the Salsa Padre at his office in the south of Santa Fe. He was an easygoing, athletic man by the name of Frank Pretto—one of the new generation of Catholic functionaries. I had been told in La Cienega that he was the person who knew Jackson best during the last years—a description which, though perhaps true, surprised the priest because he felt he had hardly known him at all. He had noticed him first as a shy old man who came to mass in La Cienega, sat at the back of the church, and slipped out quietly afterward. Because Jackson looked disheveled and drove a pickup full of brooms and shovels, Pretto assumed he was a chimney sweep.

Then one day Jackson came to the door of the trailer where Pretto lived, and having introduced himself as John, said, "Father, I love our little church, and I love the way you minister. I want you to handle my funeral, and I want to be buried in the church cemetery."

Pretto promised him that this would be done. "Is there anything else you want to tell me, John?"

"No, nothing else Father."

Jackson left, looking relieved.

Pretto asked around about him, and was told, "That old

man is well-to-do, and he has quite a background as a writer—something about gardening."

More astonishing still, Pretto learned about Jackson's relationship with La Cienega: that he had supported the community center with large annual contributions; that he had paid for a community swimming pool to be built there; that he had helped the farmers to buy their tractors; that he had employed and advised their children, often sternly, and steered them away from delinquency; that he had sent many to vocational schools and some to college, and to graduate school; that he had paid for holiday flights home from military service; that he had helped people get loans to buy and repair their houses; that he had picked up the medical bills of the sick and the dying.

One Sunday after mass, Pretto said to Jackson, "John, I didn't realize before that I was in the presence of greatness."

"You weren't, Father."

"They tell me you are a famous man."

"All that is in the past, Father."

"I want to thank you, John, for what you've done here."

"Please don't thank me."

Jackson looked so pained that Pretto never brought up the subject again. He began to wonder if something did not lurk in Jackson's past, a sin perhaps that he could not overcome.

Sitting in the parish office now, I suggested a less Catholic idea—that Jackson had consumed his life trying to understand and describe the real America, and that in the attempt he had tried to become a part of it, and that he believed now that he had failed.

This concluding part of the story is relevant to a book about the sky because it illustrates an essential aspect of the aerial view: The view is powerful and honest and worth pursuing, but it has to be nourished by the certainty of an intimate companionship—the smell, the taste, and the caress of the real life below. Jackson knew it was his childhood that kept him from finding such companionship. He rarely wrote about himself, but once in an essay entitled "The Stranger's Path," about the unkempt neighborhoods occupied by transient workers, he admitted to his own alienation from his upbringing in the better parts of town:

> In retrospect, these districts all seem indistinguishable: tree- and garden-lined avenues and lanes, curving about a landscape of hills with pretty views over other hills; the traffic becomes sparser, the houses retreat further behind tall trees and expensive flowers; every prospect is green, most prosperous and beautiful. . . . When evening falls, the softest, most domestic lights shine from upstairs windows; the only reminder of the nearby city is that dusty pink glow in the sky which in any case the trees all but conceal. Yet why have I always been glad to leave? Was it a painful realization that I was excluded from these rows and rows of (presumably) happy and comfortable homes that has always ended by making me beat a retreat to the city proper? Or was it a conviction that I had actually seen this, experienced it, relished it after a

fashion countless times and could no longer derive the slightest spark of inspiration from it?"

Jackson's problem was that when he got back to the poorer parts of town he remained a stranger there, too. His was the predicament of an aristocrat thrown forward through history, past wars and revolutions, into our peasant's democracy. Rather than retreating into preservationist fantasies—as had the polo players of Santa Fe, as well as some of his naturalist critics—Jackson had chosen instead to embrace the full turbulent force of modern American life. Still, his cherished vernacular landscape remained elusive. He tried to separate his private life from his public one, but as his writing makes grimly clear, no such separation was possible, any more than there could be an escape from self-revelation once he had set out to write about the world. *Opfer müssen gebracht werden*. Jackson had condemned himself to the stranger's path.

There were good reasons no one ever lived with him. He was a man of impractical integrity. He defined his life with successive attempts to break through to an impossible ideal, without letup, each attempt a determined escalation of the one that preceded it: the decision to leave Santa Fe for lowly La Cienega; the building of a house there with local amateur labor; the gifts to neighbors; the volunteer work on surrounding farms; the gradual shift to anonymous labor in the yards and auto shops of Santa Fe.

The job he enjoyed most was the daily cleanup at Ernie's Auto and Transmission, a filthy tin-walled garage in south

Santa Fe where he arrived every morning at six and donned a yellow hard hat before getting to work. Ernie was a friend from La Cienega who knew something of Jackson and in fondness for him left his assignments on the wall after his death:

John Jackson Duties
1. Open All Doors (Jackson had written "Help Me!" beside this.)
2. Turn On Air Compressor
3. Trash Pickup
4. Wash Floors
5. Clean Up Tools
6. Pile Up Rags
7. Clean Bathroom

For this Jackson was paid fifty dollars a week, most of which he spent on gas and dump fees. When customers complained to Ernie that he should not make an old man work so hard, Ernie did not even try to explain. When he offered to double Jackson's salary and to pick up the dump fees, Jackson refused and said, "You need me, Ernie." But after a year, when Ernie gave him a routine dollar-an-hour raise, Jackson accepted it with genuine delight. It is hard to know what he was thinking just then. Was he running out of practical ideas, giving in to magic, hoping that by acting out the motions he might yet achieve his destination? The irony, of course, is that no ordinary worker would have been so happy about the raise, so Jackson's reaction was by his own terms probably a mistake. He must have realized it afterward, too. It seems all the more remarkable that, even then, he remained a rational and reflective man, returning home every night to write about his undiminished visions.

It wasn't until nearly the end that his courage began to fail. His thinking changed, so that about when the Salsa Priest, Father Pretto, tried to thank him, he was sliding across the threshold from anticipation to despair. The "dog shit detail," which for years had served as his most hopeful experiment, now shifted underneath him, becoming more of an invited burden—an act of penance not for sin but for failure.

The change appeared one morning at Ernie's Autobody, when Jackson accidentally hosed water into a mechanic's tool chest. The mechanic went storming up to Jackson screaming, "Goddamn it John you fucking idiot, you need to watch your work! Now look what you've done!"

To Jackson at the age of eighty-six, this may have sounded like a commentary on his life. He just stood there outside Ernie's Autobody, letting the water run onto the ground, hanging his head and mumbling, "I'm sorry, sir. I'm sorry, sir. It will never happen again."

The loneliness was finally overwhelming him. He began quietly to tell people in both La Cienega and Santa Fe that he was black—an African American. For years he had attended a black Pentecostal church in Albuquerque, at first no doubt simply as an observer. Blacks were the most downtrodden people he knew of in America and therefore by his shifting definition the most vernacular—and now, if

by no better means, he would join them by bald assertion.
His friends were bewildered by Jackson's claim, but they
had grown used to what they saw as his eccentricities, and
they did not distinguish between this and his earlier, more
plausible transformations.

He saw death coming and began to attend a variety of
other Protestant churches as well. Father Pretto was unaware
of Jackson's spiritual breadth, and he later expressed surprise when I said that Jackson, as best I knew, had never
formally converted to Catholicism. He certainly had acted
like a Catholic, and had taken communion, and back in
La Cienega had never missed a Sunday at the spare little
church by the spare little cemetery. Pretto had noticed his
increasing devotion but had simply assumed that Jackson
was being a good Catholic.

But he was being more than that. The Jewish theologian
Abraham Heschel wrote that the word for "place," *makom,*
was once a synonym for God. There was something saintly
about Jackson now—a deeply personal sense not only of
place but of humility. One Sunday, during a typically
encouraging sermon on heaven and hell, Pretto became
aware that Jackson, sitting with bowed head in his habitual
place at the back of the church, had begun silently to cry.
After the service Jackson approached Pretto and with tears
still in his eyes asked, "Father, will I go to heaven?"

Pretto said, "Of course you will," because he believed it.
And because he misunderstood Jackson, he added, "If
there is anything in your past, the Lord forgives you."

But Jackson needed a second life, not forgiveness. He

had been having heart problems and was beginning to tire easily, but he refused to stop working. One Tuesday he showed up at five thirty in the morning at the house of a farmer named Ray Romero with news that his cows had gotten out. Sue Romero, in green curlers, thought he looked bad. She had worked as a nurse. She said, "John, are you taking your medicine?" He answered, "We're not here to talk about my health," and he went to work at Ernie's. By the next morning he was too sick to get up. His house-keeper found him in bed and collected some neighbors and drove him to the hospital.

That evening Ernie's mechanic son Frank went to visit him there. When Jackson saw him come into the room, he said, "Look at all these goddamned wires. Aw fuck, Frank, close that goddamned door. I just want to go home." There was no intellectualizing here and no experimenta-tion. The moment was probably as close as Jackson ever got to achieving his vernacular state of grace, but that was partly because he then died and so he could do nothing with it afterward.

Only now is his work becoming relevant to a larger audience—those of us who want to look outside in flight. It is cheap flying that brings him to us, too late for Jack-son, but not for those of us still alive, the wing-maker species just leaving the ground. Even from his motorcycle Jackson caught glimpses of the new world opening above us. These were his forays into the most human of all land-scapes—an abstraction of travel without destination, pure distilled motion, the freedom of a completely fresh relationship with space which pilots know as the inner experience of flying. Jackson wrote that we are "reestablishing a responsiveness—almost an intimacy—with a more spacious, less tangible aspect of nature. . . . The new landscape, seen at a rapid, sometimes even a terrifying pace, is composed of rushing air, shifting lights, clouds, waves, a constantly moving, changing horizon. . . . The view is no longer static; it is a revolving, uninterrupted panorama of 360 degrees." And it was as if he knew then where this book now will go. Flight's greatest gift is to let us look around, and when we do we can find ourselves reflected within the sky.

THREE

The Turn

WE FIND REFLECTIONS of ourselves there, but of all inhabited places the sky remains the strangest. Early evidence
suggested that perhaps it was meant to be so, that the sky
constituted a sacred territory, and that if God had meant
people to go there He would, for instance, have made
them lighter than air. As late as 1670—by which time it was
known that air is a gas and has weight—a Jesuit monk
named Francesco Lana who came up with an idea for a
balloon had to abandon its development for just such
philosophical reasons. Soon afterward, during Europe's
conversion to rational belief, the strictest religious doubts
faded, but questions of safety remained. Over the centuries
a number of determined travelers had equipped themselves with birdlike wings, stiffened coats, and various air

paddles, and from high towers they had bravely jumped to their deaths. It was observed that shipwrecked sailors can tread water in the ocean, cling to flotsam, and swim to the shore—but that shipwrecked "aeronauts" must fall from the sky.

This became a practical concern after two French brothers named Joseph and Etienne Montgolfier seized upon the uplifting effect of hot air. They began launching experimental unmanned balloons near Avignon in 1783. As usual in the flying business, they soon had competition. After hearing of their success, a physicist named Charles accelerated his own experiments with lighter-than-air hydrogen, and on August 27, 1783, amid much fanfare, he released an unmanned gas balloon from the center of Paris. The balloon climbed into the clouds, drifted fifteen miles downwind, and landed near the village of Gonesse— where the terrified villagers bravely attacked and shredded the monster with sickles and pitchforks.

The destruction of their competitor's balloon came as good news to the Montgolfiers. Three weeks later, following a royal banquet at Versailles, the Montgolfiers launched another hot-air balloon, again unmanned, to which however they had attached a cage carrying a rooster, a sheep, and a duck. Why these particular animals, no one knows, but the general idea was to check the effects of high altitude on living creatures. The Montgolfiers predicted that the balloon would climb to 12,000 feet and float there for twenty minutes—and that the animals would encounter there the same atmospheric conditions they would have found in the mountains at similar altitudes. In fact, the balloon reached only 1,700 feet and after a brief flight landed about a mile away. Still, the flight was thought to have been a success because all three animals had survived—though the sheep had kicked the rooster's wing. Maybe because he was more used to the aerial view, the duck had simply sat.

The Montgolfiers now set to work on a larger balloon for the first manned flight. Since they were engineers and theoreticians, and did not propose to make the flight themselves, they had to find a pilot. King Louis XVI offered to lend them a prisoner for the ride—a hapless volunteer who no doubt otherwise faced a more certain death at the king's hands. Had the Montgolfiers accepted, the first person to escape from the earth's surface would have been a convicted criminal.

No doubt aware of this, a forward-thinking young aristocrat named Pilâtre de Rozier, already well known in Parisian society for his scientific demonstrations, insisted on himself instead. On the initial tentative flights he rose just above the trees and rooftops, stoking a fire of straw and chopped wool in a hot-air balloon that, however, remained roped to the ground. Such tethered flights were, of course, too timid to justify much excitement. For the far more ambitious step of true free flight, de Rozier enlisted another young aristocrat to serve as ballast and companion and to help stoke the fire. He was a cavalry officer named the Marquis d'Arlandes, a friend of a friend of Marie Antoinette. These two—Pilâtre de Rozier and the Marquis d'Arlandes—became on November 21, 1783, the first of our species to break free of the ground. They took off before huge crowds in the Bois de Boulogne, drifted over Paris for twenty-five minutes, and after a trip of about five miles, having crossed the river Seine, landed near the present Place d'Italie.

Though the flight was a success, the big *Montgolfier* balloon suffered from a serious flaw: Its envelope was made of canvas and paper and had a dangerous tendency at its base to ignite in flight. The two airmen carried a bucket of water and extinguished the life-threatening flames with wet sponges. They did this casually by today's standards, and floated over the city as if in a dream. If the marquis' written account of the flight was admirable for its tone of Gallic nonchalance, it became heroic two years later when Pilâtre de Rozier was burned and killed in a balloon of his own design, becoming not only the first man to climb free of the earth but also the first man to die for it.

This was less important than it seemed at the time. By modern standards ballooning turned out to be a limited and impractical pursuit—not the sort of act that could take people where they wanted to go. As a result, though the first feeble moves away from the ground remain a curiosity, they lack the intellectual content that can sustain our interest now. Nonetheless, one unexpected and apparently simple observation of the human landscape still emerges from the marquis' account to lead us farther into our sky.

Naïvely, he wrote, "I was surprised at the silence and the absence of movement which our departure caused among the spectators."

What interests me here is the likelihood that the Marquis d'Arlandes was wrong. Parisian mobs are hard to impress and harder still to silence, as Louis XVI discovered a few years later. But solitary observers can be self-centered creatures, innocently assuming that others enjoy the satisfaction of their own full bellies. The marquis, it seems, had been disoriented by his sudden separation from the earth. I wonder: In his confusion did he attribute to the crowds what he himself felt—the sudden peace within the gondola, the eerie smoothness of balloon flight, its windlessness in the wind?

That sort of transposition remains today the most common illusion in the experience of flying. People on the ground know milder versions of similar reversals, observing, for example, that the sun moves toward the west, when of course it is the ground that moves toward the east. But above that, deep inside the sky, the confusion is heightened by flight's strange motions and by its utter detachment from the earth. The full extent of that detachment takes years to understand and accept. Until then balloonists continue to have the impression during takeoff not that they are climbing but that the ground crew, faces upturned, is sinking away. Airplane passengers have the impression that they are holding still, suspended in space as, far below, a miniature nation slides by. When they overtake a slower airplane they say it seems to come swimming by them backward. When another airplane passes head on in the opposite direction they comment on its startling speed. When they fly through billowing clouds they speak of the inevitability of head winds. And when in order to turn they bank to one side, expecting to feel the tilt, they find instead that the world outside has toppled in the opposite direction.

I WAS REMINDED of this one day while riding in the back of a Boeing 737 departing from San Francisco on a short flight down the coast to Los Angeles. The morning was bright. We swept up the San Francisco Bay in a gently banked left turn along the city's waterfront, out toward the Pacific. Despite the airplane's bank, most passengers peered through the windows, cautiously admiring the view. But the pilots were too enthusiastic. Directly over the Golden Gate, they rolled suddenly into a steep turn, dropping the left wing so far below the horizon that it appeared to pivot around the bridge's nearest tower. I imagine they thought of the maneuver in technical terms: We were turning already, and for just a few seconds we would exceed the airline maximum of a thirty-degree bank. The maximum is aerodynamically unimportant at cruising speeds and is imposed only for peace of mind. Sightseeing seemed more important now. The pilots probably figured they had done us a favor.

But they had not. As the airplane pivoted, the startled passengers looked away from the windows and met the eyes of their unhappy neighbors. A collective gasp rippled through the cabin. The reaction did not surprise me. Over the years I have learned never to bank steeply with my own passengers without first preparing them for the maneuver, and have noticed that even then many of them become helpless and disoriented. I do not blame them, either. As an instructor of experienced pilots, I have heard gasps and worse from my students. Pilots are merely well-trained passengers. They have to be reminded not to flinch, whimper, or make audible appeals to the Savior. They have to be encouraged to ride the airplane willingly, from the inside, and to think as it thinks. And they have to be convinced of the strange logic of the turn. At its center lies the peculiar relationship between the bank and the resulting movement of the airplane and the fact that neither can be felt. Such nothingness is what the passengers sensed when the airplane tilted over the Golden Gate— like the Marquis d'Arlandes' windlessness in the wind, an eerie lack of feeling where feeling should be.

This is the inner core of the sky that J. B. Jackson began to sense from his motorcycle but that he never really knew because he did not fly. He once wrote, "The traditional perspective, the traditional way of seeing and experiencing the world is abandoned; in its stead we become active participants, the shifting focus of a moving, abstract world; our nerves and muscles are all of them brought into play. To the perceptive individual, there can be an almost mystical quality to the experience; his identity seems for the moment to be transmuted." It was classic Jackson, compelling and open-minded and also strangely elusive. He was onto something bigger than he realized and more tangible than he could describe. For all his education, he lacked the technical knowledge—an understanding of the physics of flight, for instance—that would have allowed him to move beyond the surface of his perceptions and to give meaning to his insight. It is frustrating. I would like to have flown him through a steep turn, or through a full turning roll, and have said, "This in practice is what you mean."

Our nerves and muscles are brought into play mostly in the negative sense. The lack of feeling associated with the bank is so disorienting, so unlike experience on the ground, that many people refuse to accept it—even after they have had the turn carefully demonstrated to them. This is because they may feel the lurch as the airplane dips its wing, starting into a turn or starting out of it, and they allow this to fool them into believing that they can feel the bank itself. When the bank is visible, they ascribe their unease to fears that the airplane might slip to the side, or capsize, or somehow tumble. When the bank is not visible, during flight inside the clouds or on black nights, they no longer worry because, in their minds, that which cannot be felt does not exist.

Over history, pilots have made the same mistake. The airplane is such a simple device that it seems sometimes not to have been invented so much as discovered. Certainly the wing's profile is one of nature's purest forms. And our species was given its use before anyone knew even its most basic characteristics. Pilots as a result had to go about teaching themselves to fly. It took several generations. Eventually they had to admit that instinct abandoned them in the clouds and that they needed special instruments to tell of the bank. Without the instruments, they went into mysterious and uncontrollable turns and sometimes died. With the instruments, they maintained control and survived. Thus was born the most basic distinction in flying, between conditions in which the turn is visible and conditions in which it must be measured. And since the ability to fly through the weather has proved to be more important than speed in the conquest of distance, the mastery of the turn is the story of our sky.

The bank is a condition of tilted wings, and the turn is the change in the direction which results. The connection between the two is inexorable: The airplane must bank to turn, and when it is banked it must turn. The reason is simple. In wings-level flight, the lifting force of the wings is directed straight up, and the airplane does not turn; in a bank, the lifting force is tilted to the side, and the airplane therefore must *move* to that side. It cannot slide sideways through the air because it has a vertical fin on the tail, which forces the turn by keeping the tail in line behind the nose. The result is an elegantly curved flight path, created as the airplane lifts itself through the changes in direction.

The miraculous part of the maneuver is that the turn has an important balancing effect on the bank that causes it. The same effect, in cruder form, steadies cars on banked roadways, and bobsleds on the vertical walls of icy tracks. The difference in airplanes is that as the bank angle increases, the turn also quickens and by doing so automatically delivers a balance that is perfect. Bicycles react similarly: When they start to topple, they turn and thereby keep themselves up. Airplanes are even steadier. They operate in three-dimensional space and do not rely on tires to keep from sliding to the side. They will never capsize, no matter how steeply they are banked.

Consider for contrast the primitive banking or "heeling" of a sailboat, which does not cause a turn and which amounts to a simple trick of balancing the forces of the sail against those of the boat's ballast—whether a heavy keel or some other form of counterweight. The magnificent sensation of speed it gives is all froth and spray. The truth is, heeling slows most boats. Racers accept it as an unfortunate byproduct of the conflicting forces that allow the boat to proceed upwind. Passengers do not enjoy it in boats any more than in airplanes, but they understand it better: Heeling a boat is a thrill seeker's gambit; if it goes too far, the boat will capsize and perhaps fill with water; if people don't brace themselves, they will slide across the deck and slip into the waves. It is ironic that the physics intend boats to move on level bottoms, but require of airplanes the banked turn.

It is true that as the bank steepens in flight, directing more of the wings' lifting force into the turn, the airplane has greater difficulty holding its altitude. Flown at bank angles approaching ninety degrees—in which the wings point straight up and down—no normal airplane can keep from descending. (Some fighters can, but only because at high speeds the fuselage itself creates lift and becomes a wing.) In such "knife-edge" flight the wings exert all their lifting force in a direction parallel to the earth's surface, and gravity pulls the airplane down. But if the pilot controls the airplane carefully and allows it to keep turning, it will happily roll past the vertical, onto its back, and finally right side up again. During such a maneuver, San Francisco Bay momentarily appears *above* you, and the Golden Gate Bridge seems to hang from the water. This is fine, if you are prepared for it. Full rolls are the purest expression of flight. They are normally flown only in fighters and other acrobatic airplanes, but if you ignore convention you can safely fly them in any airplane, including a Boeing 737.

None of this would have comforted the man sitting next to me during that steep turn over the Golden Gate. He was large, sharp-eyed, and very alert. When the wing dropped, he said, "Hey!" and grabbed the armrests. Now he rode "above" me in the bank, leaning into the aisle as if he feared he might topple into my lap. He need not have worried. If he had dropped his pen, it would not have fallen "down" in the conventional sense—toward me and the earth—but rather toward the tilted carpet at his feet. If he had dangled the pen from a string, it would have hung toward the floor.

A dangled pen is a primitive inclinometer, like a plumb bob or the heel-meter of a sailboat. On land or at sea, it hangs toward the center of the planet. But in flight, it hangs toward the floor, no matter how steeply the airplane is banked. A carpenter's level would be equally fooled. This peculiar phenomenon is another manifestation of the turn's inherent balance. The earth's gravity acts normally on an airplane, but so do the forces of inertia. Inertia is the desire of any mass to keep doing what it has been doing—in an airplane, to keep moving, and moving straight. During a turn, inertia pulls horizontally. In cars, it causes people to skid off roads. In airplanes, it combines with the downward force of gravity to create a new force that pulls constantly toward the floor. Actually, the force pulls toward points in space, but by banking, the airplane places its floor directly in the way—it has to, in order to turn. The neatness of this Newtonian package is beautiful to behold. Bob Hoover, a legendary stunt pilot, used to set an empty glass on his airplane's instrument panel and pour himself a drink while flying full rolls. Our 737 pilots seemed inclined to fly the same way. If they had, as we passed through the inverted position and saw the Golden Gate Bridge hanging from the water, my sharp-eyed neighbor could have watched his pen dangling toward the sky. The flight attendants could have walked upside down. And some passengers, too self-occupied to look outside, would not have even noticed.

The human body is just another inclinometer. Undisturbed by the view, it sits quietly in its seat, dangling its feet toward the tilted floor, churning out reports for the home office. This is difficult to accept about ourselves. The inner ear, and with it any useful sense of balance, is neutralized by the motion of flight. It is our greatest weakness as fliers that, having acquired wings, we still lack an instinctive sense of bank.

For passengers this actually offers certain immediate

advantages. The man next to me, for instance, was not about to fall into my lap. He could have relaxed, lowered the tray in front of him, and called for a coffee. Unlike the table in a sailboat, an airplane tray requires no gimbals. Flight attendants brew coffee on a fixed counter, deliver it without worrying about the airplane's bank angle, and fill cups to their brims. Full cups make people behave during turns: if they try to hold them level with the earth, the coffee pours out and scalds their thighs. If this seems unusual, imagine the alternative, an airplane in which "down" was always toward the ground. Bedlam would break loose in the cabin during every turn. Unless people held their coffee just right, they would scald their neighbor's thighs.

Better to leave physics alone. As it is, as long as you contain your curiosity about what is happening outside, the inside of the cabin remains a steady and unsurprising little world. The turbulence which causes an airplane to shudder and buck is less important than people imagine. After hours on their feet, flight attendants do not develop sea legs. Passengers need no encouragement to stand and walk about. If he had stopped leaning, my neighbor could have stood up and danced the length of the tilted aisle.

THE SITUATION is not quite so carefree up front in the cockpit. In fact, the forces which tame the cabin during turns are the very same forces which over time have provided pilots with the most deadly problem of flight control. As long as its wings are level, the airplane is by nature a well-mannered animal, and slow to anger. If you pull its nose up, then release the controls, it puts its nose back down; if you push its nose down, it answers by rearing back up. Like horseback riding, flying consists mostly of leaving the beast alone, allowing it to do its own thinking. The problem is that this particular beast does not stay on the trail unguided. And once it strays, it develops a strong impulse to self-destruct.

Unguided, any airplane will eventually begin to bank. That in itself is fine if you don't mind the resulting turn, meaning the change in direction. But as the bank tilts the lift force of the wings, reducing their vertical effectiveness, it erodes the equilibrium that previously countered the pull of the earth. The airplane responds to the loss by lowering its nose and accelerating. Sitting in the cockpit with folded arms and watching it proceed is like sitting on a temperamental horse and letting it gallop down a steepening slope: It requires a morbid curiosity and steady nerves. In flight, the slope steepens because the acceleration tightens the airplane's turn, which increases its bank angle, which causes further acceleration. A sort of aerodynamic lock-in occurs. The airplane banks to the vertical or beyond and points its nose straight down.

That is the spiral dive. In its most virulent form pilots sometimes call it the graveyard spiral. The airplane descends in ever steeper circles and either disintegrates in mid-air from the air pressures of excessive speed or shatters against the ground at the bottom of a screaming descent. All fights would suffer this end if the pilot (or autopilot) did not intervene.

In good weather the intervention is easy. You hold the controls lightly, and when you see that the airplane has banked, you unbank it. During turns you hold the controls more firmly and keep the nose from dropping. The increased loading created by inertia during such a well-flown turn is felt within the airplane as a peculiar heaviness—a "pull" not toward the ground, of course, but toward the cabin floor. Pilots measure it in "Gs," as a multiple of gravity's normal pull on the surface of the earth, or in steady wings-level flight. An airplane that banks to thirty degrees, the airline standard, creates a loading of 1.15 Gs: The airplane, and everything in it, temporarily weighs fifteen percent more than normal. Fifteen percent is just barely noticeable. But only a bit steeper, at a forty-five-degree bank, the load increases to 1.4 Gs: People feel pressed into their seats, and if they look outside they may notice that the wings have flexed upward. Technically, such loadings are not important. Airplanes are strong and flexible, and pilots shrug off 2 Gs and may feel comfortable at twice as much. But passengers are unaccustomed to the sensation. As we pivoted over the Golden Gate, the man in the seat beside me suddenly gained about eighty pounds. Had he dangled his pen toward the tilted floor, it would have pulled on the string with surprising force. This might not have reassured him. But the extra heaviness was a measure of the pilot's success in resisting the spiral dive. If we had felt "normal" during the turn, it could only have meant that the nose was dropping fast toward the water.

No pilot would make such a mistake on a clear day. The view from the cockpit is dominated by the horizon, the constantly renewing division between the sky and the earth. It forms a line across the windshield and makes immediate sense of the airplane's movements. Birds, too, use the horizon. The sight of an angled and shifting world must act powerfully on them. They are subject to the same laws of physics as airplanes, but they fly with insouciance, neither worrying about their inability to feel the bank nor pondering the explosive nature of the spiral dive. They can get away with this not because they are better fliers than we— in truth, they are worse—but because they can wait out bad weather and usually do. People do not have that luxury. We fly on schedules, through clouds and storms and across the blackest nights. When no useful horizon is visible outside the cockpit we maintain control of the airplane by reference to an artificial horizon on the instrument panel. And so we outdo the birds.

But the use of that tool is not as obvious as it might at first seem. The artificial horizon is a gyroscopically steadied line which stays constantly level with the earth's surface. The airplane pitches and banks in relation to this steady line, which in spatial terms never moves. The problem is, in *airplane* terms it does move. And pilots are part of the airplane—they fly it from within, strapped to their seats, sensing like the Marquis d'Arlandes their own full bellies. In clear skies they would never misjudge a bank as the tilting of the earth, but with their view restricted to the abstractions of the instrument panel they sometimes do just that: They perceive the airplane's lateral motion as a movement on the face instrument of the artificial horizon line. This causes them to "fly" the wrong thing—the

moving horizon line, rather than the fixed symbolic airplane. For example, as turbulence banks the airplane to the
left, the pilots, banking with it, notice the artificial horizon
line dropping to the right. Reacting instinctively to the
indication of motion, they try to raise the line as if it were
a wing. The result of such a reversal is murderous. Pilots
steer to the left just when they should steer to the right,
and then in confusion they steer harder. While maneuvering calmly inside the clouds, I have flown with students
who for this reason suddenly tried to flip my airplane
upside down. They were rational people, confronted by
the turn.

It is the sort of concrete experience that J. B. Jackson
sought and was never able to find. We are the energetic,
self-centered, adaptable species, carving a landscape of
motion through the sky. If we try to fly by instinct through
the weather, even the best of us will roll into spiral dives.
And if we misread an artificial horizon, or follow one that
has failed, we will take a shortcut to the same destination.
The circumstance that causes the spiral is the very circumstance that prevents its solution. The bank itself cannot be
felt. Pilots experience the fury of the dive and die in confusion. That is the inside history of human flight. The
Montgolfier brothers gave us the balloon and introduced
us to the peculiar egotism of flight. The Wright brothers
gave us the wing and confronted us with the dilemma of
the turn.

*　　*　　*

THE WRIGHTS flew straight and level at Kitty Hawk, North Carolina, on December 17, 1903, and a bewildered press paid little attention. The flight was the culmination of an almost incredible four-year story—two unassuming bicycle builders engaged in a process of problem solving so sure-footed that it left the world behind. The Wright brothers were simply smarter than their peers—much smarter. If their insight was to understand the importance of flight control, it was only with the mastery of the bank that they achieved their purpose. After their initial straight-ahead runs, they went home to Ohio, rented a cow pasture on the trolley line outside of Dayton, and spent the following year stretching their flights and learning to turn. At a time when higher authorities continued to proclaim that such acts were impossible, deep in the American country-side there were a few farmers who came quietly to know that the Wright brothers could fly.

The first detailed account of the Wrights' success appeared not in the New York *Times* or the *Scientific American,* but in *Gleanings in Bee Culture,* a little magazine for beekeepers published in Medina, Ohio. The editor and publisher was Amos Root, a typically moralistic Midwest-erner with a taste for practical technology. In an aside intended as a parallel to the Wrights' experience, he admitted that as a young man he had imported the first modern bicycle to Ohio.

The whole town jeered at me, and the story of the "fool and his money" was hurled in my teeth so many times I almost dread to hear it even yet. Men of good fair understanding pointed their fingers at me, and said that anybody of good common sense ought to know that *that* thing would not stand up with a man on it, for that would be an utter impossibility. . . . Finally I rented the largest hall in the town, went in with one trusty boy who had faith, for a companion, and *locked the door.* After quite a little practice on the smooth floor of the hall I succeeded in riding from one end to the other; but I could not turn the corners. When, after still more practice, I did turn one corner without falling, how my spirits arose! A little later I went in a wabbly way clear around the room. Then my companion did the same thing, and, oh how we did rejoice and gather faith! A little later on, with a flushed but happy face, I went out into the street and rode around the public square.

Thirty years later now, Amos Root had a car, which he drove 350 miles round trip to visit the Wrights' cow pasture near Dayton. There on September 20, 1904, he happened to witness Wilbur fly the airplane's first full circle.

Bees, of course, are the great specialists of full-circle flying; they spend their days on round-trip missions and construct whole landscapes out of their ability to turn. Root must have been influenced by that knowledge. It is clear that he felt a general enthusiasm for circular movement, which meant that he of all people was predisposed to appreciate the significance of the flight that day. He labeled it "the first successful trip of an airship, without balloon to sustain it, that the world has ever made, that is, to turn the corners and come back to the starting-point." And he was right. It is the turn that makes the airplane practical.

The U.S. Army was slower to catch on. Five years later, after much convincing by the Wrights, it reluctantly took delivery of its first airplane. In 1909, horses still seemed more glorious. The war in Europe changed that. By its end in 1918, the cavalry had been slaughtered, and flying was all that remained of chivalry and adventure. Unsullied by the carnage in the trenches, pilots chased across the sky, turning hard on each other's tails. The war taught them to fly with confidence and encouraged among them the myth of inborn ability. They called it flying by the seat of the pants.

As in all wars since, more pilots died by error than by enemy action. Those who died in spiral dives left no records. Those who survived made the dangerous discovery that people can feel at home in the sky. They learned to accept the strangeness of a steep bank—the G-load and the sight of a tilted horizon—and the magic of a full roll. Nonetheless, they still believed in balance. When they ducked through small clouds and emerged with their wings slightly tilted, they did not suspect the importance of the unfelt bank. Luckily for them, when the weather was bad, or on black nights, they waited on the ground. German pilots called good conditions "flight weather," because they could fly, and bad conditions "flier's weather," because they could stay in bed. By happy coincidence, pilots had no reason to fly when they had nothing to see.

After the war, regular airmail service started in Europe and the United States. It made airplanes useful to the public for the first time, gave birth to the airlines, and placed pressure on the pilots to operate on schedules. They followed rivers and railroads in open cockpit biplanes with no gyroscopic instruments and flew under the weather, sometimes at extremely low altitude, dodging steeples and oil derricks.

One of those early airmail pilots, Dean Smith, wrote about getting his first route briefing for a bad weather run, west across the Allegheny Mountains to Cleveland:

From the field here at Bellefonte you head west through the gap in the ridge. Climb as you veer a bit north, passing over the center of this railroad switchback up the side of Rattlesnake Mountain, then due west again to clear the top of the ridge at, say, 2,200 feet. After about ten miles you hit the railroad again at Snow Shoe—look sharp, it's only four or five houses—then follow the railroad on down to the other side of the Rattlesnake to the valley where you pick up the West Branch of the Susquehanna River, winding along to the town of Clearfield, which you will know by three round water reservoirs just south of town. Next, you have to get over about thirty miles of plateau to Du Bois. This is pretty high, about 2,200 feet, but it is fairly smooth on top and there is a white gravel road cut through the trees straight to Du Bois. As you come into town you will see the railroad to your right, and just south of the railroad a piece of flat pasture you can land on in a pinch. Then the highway leads you for fifty miles through Brookville to Clarion. Each of these towns has a half-mile race track. The one at Clarion is half full of trees, but the one at Brookville is clean and hard, and it's the best emergency field from here to Cleveland: as soon as you land you will be met by a girl named Alice Henderson, driving a big Cadillac, who will be pleased to look after you. After Clarion, the country gradually gets lower until you cross the Allegheny at Greenville, which you can identify by a big S bend in the river. From then on it's clear sailing.

After such a flight, no one could accuse a pilot of not having "been" to the mountains. Many were killed for the attempt; in fact, the early airmail flying was the most dangerous flying the world has ever known. But still the globe refused to shrink. Fog, night, and heavy weather continued to ground the airplanes. Some pilots did have a rough, though technically uninformed, respect for the disorientation lurking deep within the clouds, but most pilots simply stayed below the weather. In pride and ignorance they told themselves that this was because without radio navigation they needed to see landmarks to find their way. It was another happy coincidence.

In the winter of 1925, a young Army pilot named Carl Crane got caught in the clouds at 8,000 feet directly over Detroit while trying to fly a congressman's son to Washington, D.C., in a biplane. Crane later became a famous master of the turn. Speaking of the flight, he said,

In a short time, I was losing altitude, completely out of control. I could not fly the airplane at all—it had gotten into a spiral dive. Half way down I looked around at my boy in the back, and he was enjoying the flight no end. He was shaking his hands and grinning, and I was slowly dying because I knew we were going to crash.

The boy in the rear cockpit was just unaware. Crane had an altimeter and airspeed indicator. He thought he was dying "slowly" only because of the way experience is compressed when an airplane goes wild. Pilots then tend not to think about God or their lives but about solutions. Once when flying a series of ill-considered acrobatic maneuvers, I stupidly lost control of an airplane and started into a flat spin—a dangerous condition from which there may be no recovery. On that particular flight a video camera had been mounted behind me in the cockpit, and as a result I later saw the whole thing on tape: the nose rising unexpectedly, the forested horizon swirling, and the uninformed attempt to find the answer—the systematic control stick motions, the experimental bursts of power, the reach for the canopy jettison knob, the inexplicable return to normal flight. The experience was frightening, even though I was wearing a parachute and flying in the clear. But what surprised me most about it later, when I saw it in on the tape, was the speed with which it was over.

Carl Crane's loss of control, which was both more dangerous and more prolonged, must have seemed at the time to stretch on for an eternity. Neither he nor his passenger was wearing a parachute. From his training he remembered only vague admonitions to stay out of the weather. But he was in the weather now and couldn't see a thing. He knew he was turning but could make no sense of the compass. It is a notorious problem: Because the earth's magnetic field does not lie parallel to the globe's surface but dips down toward the magnetic poles, the compass card responds to banks by spinning erratically, jamming, and sometimes showing turns in reverse. Crane did not know which wing was down, let alone by how much. If he tried to level the wings, he was just as likely to roll upside down as right side up. If he tried to raise the nose, the effect would be to quicken the turn and steepen the dive. Crane understood none of the details at the time, but he sensed that his situation was hopeless.

Dean Smith, the early airmail pilot, had gone through a similar experience. His memoir of a weather flight, written thirty years later, still rings with the authentic confusion of the time:

> Now followed a long period of fighting to keep control of the plane while all the time my equilibrium became steadily more confused. I succeeded in climbing to 8,000 feet; then the plane began to get more and more out of control. It lost altitude until I was back down to 5,000 feet. . . . At last I fell. The plane stalled and whipped off into a spin, although to my bewildered senses it did not seem to be spinning down, but impossibly up and to the side. I cut the

throttle and held the plane in the spin for a few seconds to be certain I was in a known condition and to force my mind to reorient. When I broke the spin, I couldn't pull out level from the resulting dive. By the time I got the wires to stop screaming the plane promptly stalled again. The plane floundered through the dark muck in a series of stalls, spins, dives, and pull-outs. I struggled and fought with it all the way down, working with desperate concentration, but that little corner of my mind that detachedly views such things said, "My friend, you are a dead duck."

Dean Smith happened to survive, but others even today do not. The physics have not changed. In modern times, air traffic control recorded the radio transmissions of an unskilled pilot who, with family on board, tried to descend through an overcast. After he lost control, he began to sob into the microphone, begging the radar controllers to tell him which side was up. But radar shows air traffic as wingless blips on an electronic map, and is incapable of distinguishing banks. Controllers are in the business of keeping airplanes from colliding. Pilots are in the business of flight control. This one had instruments on board by which he could have kept his wings level, but in the milkiness of the clouds he became confused. The controllers listened helplessly to his panic and, in the background, to the screams of his children. The transmission ended when the airplane broke apart, somewhere far away inside the sky.

But Carl Crane's biplane—over Detroit in 1925 with the congressman's son—was stronger:

Finally it got down to under a thousand feet, and I said, "Well here we go. I'm going to look at my boy once more." And as I turned around to look at him, a sign went by my wing. It said "Statler Hotel." I had just missed the top of the Statler Hotel. In all the mist and rain, I could see the buildings and the streets. I flew down the street and got over the Detroit River, and flew down about ten feet high all the way to Toledo, shaking all the way.

Crane became obsessed. Shocked by the way intuition had abandoned him, he began to ask questions. For years he got no intelligent answers. He never met Dean Smith. Those veterans he did meet kept insisting they could fly by the seat of their pants, and they thought less of those who could not. Their self-deception now seems all the more profound because the solution—a gyroscope adapted to flying—was already widely available.

THE GYROSCOPE is a spinning wheel, like a child's top, mounted in gimbals that allow it freedom of movement. It has two important traits: Left alone, it maintains fixed orientation in space (in relation to the stars); and when tilted, it reacts in an odd but predictable way. Elmer Sperry, the great American inventor, started playing with these traits in the early 1900s. As a curiosity, he designed a gyro-stabilized "trained wheelbarrow," and he tried, without success, to interest a circus in it. Undiscouraged, Sperry turned to the

U.S. Navy instead and interested it in gyro-compasses and ship stabilizers. Competitors in Europe developed similar devices and during the buildup to war interested their countries' navies, too.

Airplanes were an intriguing sideline. Sperry built a gyroscopic autopilot in 1910, not to enable blind flight but to stabilize the otherwise unruly early flying machines. In 1915 he began to ponder instrumentation and with prescient insight into the problems of flight was able after three years to produce the first gyroscopic turn indicator, an instrument still in use today. Its face consisted of a vertical pointer, which indicated turns to the left or right. (Necessarily, it also included a ball like a carpenter's level, an inclinometer that showed not bank but "skid" or "slip"—conditions of lateral imbalance.) Sperry called the instrument a "crutch to the compass." In his patent application he described its use as an instrument that would allow pilots to fly indefinitely through the clouds, implying that without it they could not.

It was hardly a secret. Already by the end of World War I, thinkers on both sides of the Atlantic had understood the difficulties of the banked turn, but the great majority of professional pilots continued to disdain the idea of any crutch. A group of Sperry's employees split off and, calling themselves the Pioneer Instrument Company, went into production with the device. They found the market difficult. For the next twenty years customers kept complaining to them about a mysterious problem: The instruments worked just fine in clear air, but as soon as they were taken into clouds they began to indicate turns.

Not all pilots were that stupid. One of the first cloud flights with this new device, the turn indicator, was made in 1918 by William Ocker, an Army captain and an experienced aviator. Though Ocker, too, lost control and spiraled out of the overcast, he assumed that the error was his, and he set off on an eleven-year quest for good answers.

During the 1920s a few of the more progressive airmail pilots, operating under deadly pressure to push the weather, began to admit the need to control their bank angles by reference to the instruments. Charles Lindbergh was one of those converts. When he crossed the Atlantic in 1927, he used a turn indicator with which he had first experimented only months before, and he readily admitted afterward that it had kept him from spiraling into the sea. His description of that historic piece of instrument flying holds true today:

What lies outside doesn't matter. My world and my life are compressed within these fabric walls. Flying blind is difficult enough in smooth air. In this swirling cloud, it calls for all the concentration I can muster. The turn and bank indicators, the air speed, the altimeter, and the compass, all those phosphorescent lines and dots in front of me, must be kept in proper place. When a single one strays off, the rest go chasing after it like so many sheep, and have to be caught quickly and carefully herded back into position again.

Two years later, in 1929, a young military pilot and engineer from MIT named James Doolittle made a "blind" landing after flying a complete circuit around an airport in a special biplane modified with a domed cockpit from which he could not see outside. The landing itself was a technical dead end. Once Doolittle was over the field he reduced the power and waited until the biplane plunked onto the grass—an impractical technique for airlines then or now. More significant were the special devices that made the precisely flown circuit possible. The airplane was equipped with navigational radios, an airspeed indicator, an improved altimeter, a turn indicator, and two new gyroscopic instruments which Sperry's son, also named Elmer, had developed with Doolittle's guidance—a gyroscopic compass and an artificial horizon. This combination was so effective that it still forms the core of instrument panels today. Doolittle reported that using the artificial horizon was "like cutting a porthole through the fog to look at the real horizon." But that was the easy part. There remained the more stubborn problem of belief.

Marked for life by his near collision with the Statler Hotel, Carl Crane read the descriptions of Doolittle's 1929 flight with fascination. He was now an Army instructor at a training base near San Antonio, Texas. Though his superior officers disapproved of instrument flying, Crane was convinced of the need for gyroscopes. He finally got permission to cover over a cockpit and turn one of the biplanes into an instrument trainer. While he was at work on this, William Ocker wandered into the hangar.

Ocker was the man who had lost control of his airplane while flying with one of Sperry's first turn indicators back in 1918—and he had been worrying about it ever since. He didn't look like much of a pilot, with his bifocals and his mournful puritan's face, but he had a powerful mind and all the conviction of a missionary. The truth about instrument flying had come to him in 1926, during a standard medical examination at Crissy Field in San Francisco. Part of the routine was a crude test of balance involving the use of a Barany chair, a rotating seat on which the pilot spun with closed eyes. Ocker easily passed the required test, but afterward the examining doctor, who was an old friend, told him that he would now demonstrate to him that his senses could indeed be fooled. This time Ocker felt the chair begin to turn, and he guessed the direction correctly—but when the chair slowed, he felt that it had stopped, and when it stopped, he felt that it had started to turn in the opposite direction.

For the doctor the demonstration was a parlor game, a gentle amusement with the inner ear. For William Ocker, however, it amounted to a stunning revelation: The sense of accelerating into a turn is the same as that of decelerating from the opposite turn. Here at last was the explanation for the persistence of so much confusion and death. The chair had induced the same false sensation that eight years before had caused him to lose control while flying with the turn indicator and that still today was leading even those few pilots who accepted their inability to feel the bank to distrust their instruments and roll for no apparent reason into dangerous spiral dives.

It was a moment to equal the Wright brothers' first full

circle. The story goes that Ocker said nothing but left the doctor's office, went immediately to his airplane, and retrieved his personal portable air-driven turn indicator, which he proceeded to rig up inside a shoe box. He cut a viewing hole into one end of the box, attached a penlight and a black fabric hood to it, and returned that afternoon to the office, where he challenged his friend the doctor to trick him again—with the difference that this time he would look into the shoe box. Again Ocker experienced the false sensations, but because he refused to believe them and relied exclusively on the turn indicator, he could not be fooled. The doctor could hardly have grasped the significance of what he was seeing, but there on his simple spinning chair the bespectacled pilot William Ocker was giving birth to modern instrument flying. He had discovered the most disturbing limitation of human flight—that instinct is *worse* than useless in the clouds, that it can induce deadly spirals, and that as a result having gyroscopes is not enough, that pilots must learn against all contradictory sensations the difficult discipline of an absolute belief in their instruments. Perhaps equally as important, he had invented a way to prove it.

Ocker became so obsessed with the spinning chair that the Army hospitalized him twice for sanity tests, then banished him to Texas. Still he refused to quit. When Ocker met Crane in the hangar in Texas, he invited him for a spin in a revolving chair, and then and there Crane became Ocker's disciple. The two men began a joint exploration of all known aspects of flight inside the clouds. In 1932 they published *Blind Flight in Theory and Practice,* the first systematic analysis of instrument flying. It was dedicated, no doubt with some bitterness, "To those courageous airmen who have risked criticism and loss of professional prestige by precisely relating their own difficult experiences during bad weather flight."

The book had an enormous influence, though more at first with the Russians than with the U.S. Army Air Corps, which adopted it as a training text only at the outbreak of World War II. Never mind. The authors effectively laid to rest the old faith in flying by instinct. They described the physics of the turn and the confusion experienced by the inner ear, but their most dramatic argument grew out of an experiment with pigeons. From everything humans had learned after three decades of winged flight, it now seemed likely that birds, too, must be unable to fly without a visible horizon. Ocker and Crane decided to find out. They acquired a few pigeons, blindfolded them, took them up in biplanes, and threw them out. Sure enough the birds dropped into fluttering emergency descents—they panicked and went down like feathered parachutes. It is possible, of course, that they did not like the blindfolds, which were made of Bull Durham tobacco pouches. But anyway, the experiment was the kind pilots could understand. If God had meant birds to fly in the clouds, He would have given them gyroscopes.

BIRDS CANNOT FLY through heavy rain. They get sucked up by thunderstorms, frozen by altitude, and burned by lightning. They lose control and crash, fly into obstacles, wander offshore, drift off course, get hopelessly lost, run out of fuel, and die by the millions. They would rather not migrate in bad weather, and they usually don't. Nonetheless, it appears that Ocker and Crane may have been wrong. There is evidence now that perhaps some birds do occasionally fly inside the clouds.

This is big news, though as time has shown it is not news of the sort that people seek out. Word of it first appeared back in 1972, in the proceedings of a NASA symposium on animal navigation. Hidden among reports like "When the Beachhopper Looks at the Moon" and "Anemomenotactic Orientation in Beetles and Scorpions" (When a Bug Feels the Wind) was a paper entitled "Nocturnal Bird Migration in Opaque Clouds." It was written by Donald Griffin, a Harvard zoologist who earlier had discovered the use of sonar by bats. Griffin reported that he had borrowed a military radar and on overcast nights in New York had tracked birds that seemed to be flying *inside* the clouds. There were only a few such birds, and Griffin was able to track them only for a couple of miles, but they appeared to be proceeding under control.

Griffin's biggest problem was uncertainty over the precise flight conditions at the birds' altitude. Was the weather really as thick as it looked from below? Were the birds really flying blind? Griffin had good reasons to believe so, but as a scientist he had to be cautious. His final report, in 1973, reinforced the earlier findings but was more carefully entitled "Oriented Bird Migration in or between Opaque Cloud Layers."

To ornithologists interested in bird navigation, the difference between "in" and "between" seems to be an unimportant detail—their concentration being instead on the observation that Griffin's birds could apparently find their way without reference to the stars or the ground. But to the birds, whose first job—like that of pilots—must be to control their bank angles, the distinction might be crucial. The ornithologists seem not to know that they should care, as if for all their curiosity about the birds' earthly habitats, the issue of the spiral dive has never even entered their minds. Griffin, a former pilot, understands the issue's importance. I once sought him out and expressed my frustration that so many ornithologists seem to be stuck on the ground. He laughed. "I keep telling them, 'Gee, birds fly!'"

Assuming they fly in the clouds, the question is, How? Ornithologists have no answer, and they shy away from speculation. It is known that birds navigate by watching the ground and the positions of the sun, the moon, and the stars—none of which would help them maintain control in the clouds. But they may also use a host of nonvisual clues and may use mental "maps" based on sound, smell, air currents, variations in gravitational pull, and other factors. Experiments have shown that some species are extremely sensitive to magnetic forces. The heads of these species contain magnetite crystals surrounded by nerves, which may give them an intuitive knowledge of their direction (and possibly location) in the earth's magnetic field. A highly refined and error-free sense of direction, or of *change* in direction, could in theory amount to a non-gyroscopic turn indicator—a biological crutch for winged flight in the clouds.

The other possibility is that some birds actually do have gyroscopes of a primitive sort. This is less far-fetched than it seems. The rhythmic flapping of wings could have the effect of Foucault's pendulum, allowing a bird to sense turns without any external cue. A pendulum is more than a hanging weight; it is a hanging weight that has been pushed and is swinging freely. Swinging gives the pendulum its special ability to maintain spatial orientation. Leon Foucault was the French physicist who first used one, in 1851, to demonstrate the rotation of the earth: Though the pendulum appeared to change its direction as it swung, in fact the plane of its motion remained constant, and the apparent change was caused by the turning of the earth underneath it. Foucault knew that a spinning wheel would possess the same properties of spatial orientation, and though he never perfected such a device (largely because he could not figure out how to drive it), he coined the term "gyroscope" for it—from the Greek *gyros,* for "rotation," and *skopeein,* for "viewing."

If birds do rely on the pendulum effect in some sense to "see" through the clouds, they are not alone. Flies and mosquitoes (among more than 85,000 other species of Diptera) use specially adapted vibrating rods to maintain spatial orientation in flight. Not only can they turn sharply, roll inverted, and land on the underside of leaves, but they can do it in a fog.

Pilots, too, have relied on pendulums. It is said that an airliner inbound to New York in the 1950s lost all its gyroscopes in heavy weather over Block Island. The captain was a wise old man who had risen with the airlines from the earliest airmail days and was now approaching retirement. A lesser pilot might have fallen for the trap of intuition. But the captain simply took out his pocket watch, dangled it from its chain, and began to swing it toward the instrument panel. Flying by the pendulum and the compass, he proceeded the length of Long Island in the clouds. After breaking into the clear near the airport, he landed and wished his passengers a good day.

The story is not impossible. It came to mind one night when I flew out over the Pacific Ocean, off the coast of Oregon, alone at the controls of a borrowed single-engine airplane. High clouds darkened the sky. The light of a lonely fishing boat drifted by below. Flying a mile above the water, I headed beyond the boat and into the complete blackness of approaching weather. It was an experience of Jacksonian solitude: in dark clouds over a wild ocean, an absolute night, the cockpit a world of its own, the instrument panel a landscape within it. The instruments glowed in a warm light, abstracting the strange story of flight's pure motion.

The gyroscopes functioned perfectly. The radios were blissfully silent. I hooked a metal pen to a fishing line and dangled it from a knob on the ceiling. Flying by the artificial horizon, I made a steep turn and watched the pen dangle toward the tilted floor. Then I straightened out, pushed the pen toward the instrument panel, and released it. It swung for almost thirty seconds before requiring another push. The problem, of course, was that each renewal would erase the pendulum's spatial memory. Nonetheless, I thought the device might work. After turning north, the direction in which the compass is most confused by the bank, I covered the gyroscopes with slips of paper.

The night air was smooth. The pen swung rhythmically toward the panel and back. Eventually it redirected itself to the left. This could only have meant that the airplane had banked and turned to the right. I rolled to the left gingerly, hoping to raise the right wing just enough to return to straight flight. The pen seemed to stabilize in its new direction. I renewed the swing, shoving the pen again directly toward the panel. It soon confirmed that the airplane had indeed leveled its wings and stopped turning. The compass settled, showing that earlier I had strayed twenty degrees to the right. Lowering the left wing cautiously, watching the pen swing to the right, I crept back to the original heading. Later, when I tried to make a large turn, I lost control and spiraled and had to peek at the gyroscopes. But with the wings level again, I flew on for miles, learning to work with the swinging pen. Trust comes slowly in the indication of turns. It is a small faith that allows us to fly so deeply into the sky.

FOUR

On a Bombay Night

THIS IS A STORY about that faith. On another black night, at the end of the first day of 1978, a Boeing 747 with 213 people aboard taxied for takeoff at the airport in Bombay, the great port city on India's western coast. The airplane belonged to Air India and was operating as Flight 855 bound for Dubai, an oil-rich city of the United Arab Emirates, where many of the passengers worked. In its belly it carried a cargo of betel leaves, a mild stimulant chewed by Indian laborers and destined in this case for the homesick expatriates of the Arabian Peninsula.

The night sky over Bombay was clear, moonless, and hazy with smoke from the city. A balmy ocean breeze blew across the airport from the nearby Arabian Sea. The Boeing had arrived from New York the day before and had flown on a local training mission, during which it had struck a bird, damaging the right wing's leading edge. Twelve hours late now because of the subsequent repairs, it moved into position at the head of Bombay's main west-facing runway.

The man in command was Captain V. I. Kukar, at age fifty a senior pilot who had logged nearly 18,000 flight hours during twenty-two years with the airline. His co-pilot I. Virmari, age forty-three, was also highly experienced. Slightly behind them sat a man named Faria, age fifty-three, the flight engineer, whose job was to look after the 747's intertwined and redundant operating systems. Tonight all the systems looked good. The airplane was light and had ample margins of performance. Despite the size of the cabin that trailed behind it, the cockpit itself was a contained and intimate place, glowing in the warm lights of the instrument panels and not appreciably different from the cockpits of less imposing airplanes. The crew must have felt entirely at home there.

They expected to reach their initial cruising altitude of 31,000 feet by following a standard departure procedure known as the "Seaweed One," which called for them after crossing the coastline to make a gentle right turn and climb away from Bombay over the night ocean.

Cleared for takeoff just before 8:09 PM, the big, well-lit Boeing rumbled down the runway and lifted gracefully into the sky. Captain Kukar was at the controls. He held the airplane's nose a bit lower than usual, possibly for the pleasure of a good acceleration, and called in sequence for the landing gear and flap retractions. At 8:11 the Bombay departure controller spotted Flight 855 on radar and asked it to report passing through 8,000 feet.

Kukar answered, "Happy New Year to you, sir. Will report leaving eight-zero, 855." He was a mile offshore, climbing through 1,200 feet and rolling smoothly into the expected right turn, doing about 280 miles per hour. It was his last radio transmission. Twenty-two seconds later he and everyone else on board hit the water and died.

Air India 855 dove steeply and at high speed into the Arabian Sea. A great number of Bombay citizens were outdoors enjoying the evening air and mingling along the shore, and many of them saw the airplane fall. We can understand why their impressions were confused. If it is hard to believe that something as massive as a 747 can lift into the sky, it is harder still to accept, once it is engaged in forward flight, that something so stately and certain might come plunging back down. Many years later and on the other side of the world, this is what bewildered the observers of TWA's catastrophic 747 fuel tank explosion off New York. The fireball in the sky seemed to have been caused by a missile fired from the surface, not only because the flaming fuselage soared momentarily upward, but also because the mind required some such immediate explanation for what could only have been the unthinkable reality of a great airplane going down.

Air India went down much closer to the shore—so close that people clearly heard the boom of the impact. At least one witness believed that a meteor had fallen. Others saw the airplane explode in flight, or plunge in a streak of fire, or explode on impact, or slip fully intact beneath the waves. It was all over so very quickly. Afterward the sea lay as black and untroubled as it had lain before. The wonder is that a few witnesses actually did understand what had happened, as the subsequent investigation verified, and that they were able to describe with some precision the external appearance of the accident: the proud flight passing overhead and climbing offshore, the beginnings of the shallow right turn, then the strange reversal—the sharp roll to the left, and the dive at impossibly steep bank angles into the ocean.

The newspapers naturally speculated on the possibility of sabotage and political terrorism. An anonymous letter described a conspiracy involving counterfeit dollars and a bomb in the betel leaves. But as the Indian Navy began to salvage pieces of the airplane, the investigators found no signs of fire, heat, or inflight breakup. The airplane's crash-proof "black boxes," the flight-data and cockpit-voice recorders whose purpose is to provide a history of the details leading to an accident, were recovered intact. They indicated that the airplane's engines and controls had functioned normally, but that—on the basis of the recorded conversations and control wheel positions—something in the cockpit had gone terribly wrong. The fault appeared to be Kukar's. On a quiet night in Bombay after twenty-two years of steady service he had flown a perfectly good airplane into the water.

*   *   *

KUKAR WAS FLYING by the big artificial horizon in front
of him, the so-called attitude director indicator, or ADI.
The copilot, whose tasks included monitoring the captain's flying, had his own independent artificial horizon. At
the center of the instrument panel, easily visible to both
pilots, was a smaller standby horizon, which also was independent. In addition, each pilot had a gyroscopic compass and turn indicator, along with the standard clusters of
nongyroscopic instruments—airspeed, altimeter, and vertical speed, among others. Over history these instruments
have been steadily consolidated in an effort to reduce the
difficulty of the pilot's visual scan—the ghostly "herding"
that kept Lindbergh busy during his flight across the
Atlantic. Nonetheless, even in the most recent "glass" cockpits with their crisp and minimalistic displays, the instruments have changed surprisingly little since those first
developed by Sperry and Doolittle in the open-cockpit
biplanes of the 1920s. For all its apparent complexity,
Kukar's 747 panel was largely just an answer to every
biplane's needs.

What *has* changed is the way the instruments are used.
Flight in the early years was an immediate and tactile experience, a short step away from the ground, and it required
instrumentation only during passage through the clouds.
Flight in a jet is a more distant experience and a condition
more completely of the sky. Isolated not only by the quiet
of the cockpit but by climb performance and high cruising
altitudes, pilots are taught to "fly the numbers" and to rely
on their instruments for all stages of flight. The amateur-
ish distinction between visual and instrument conditions,

like the antique one between "flight weather" and "flier's weather," seems hardly to matter anymore. Airplanes shrug off most weather. And we have come to a time when the least curious (and usually least competent) pilots hardly bother to look outside at all except during takeoff and landing. Even so, the physics of flights have not changed. The bank still cannot be felt. When it also cannot be seen outside the airplane, even peripherally, it must still be treated with great care—measured and controlled on the inside with gyroscopes. Ocker and Crane are long forgotten. Working pilots now accept their teachings as their own. But when it comes to a showdown, some still fall apart.

Kukar's trouble started when he began the right turn, at about the same time he wished the departure controller a happy New Year. The airplane was still heading west, into the blackout conditions of the night sky. A moment later, according to the flight-data recorder, Kukar made an unnecessary and unusually large control wheel movement to the left. The airplane answered appropriately by rolling out of the right bank, passing through wings-level flight, and dipping into a left turn. Kukar must have thought he was still turning to the right, because he now steered the control wheel even farther to the left. The airplane's left bank angle passed through thirty degrees, and the nose began to drop, flattening the climb. All this happened in three seconds.

Kukar knew something was wrong. The cockpit-voice recorder picked up the surprise in his voice. He swore, *"Arey Yar!"* and said, "My instrument!"

His "instrument" was of course Sperry's device, the all-important artificial horizon.

Kukar brought the control wheel back to neutral—a position to which the airplane would have responded, if only temporarily, by holding a steady bank angle. But Kukar was confused. Again he steered hard to the left.

The copilot looked down at his own artificial horizon, and saw the indication of a steep and unexpected left bank. He said, "My . . . Mine's . . ."

Kukar said, "Mine's just . . ."

The copilot said, "Mine's is also toppled!"

Kukar said, "Check your instrument!"

This conversation took four seconds, during which Kukar continued to swing the control erratically to the left. Though he did not know it, the airplane was banking past seventy degrees and accelerating through 300 miles per hour, and the nose was dropping swiftly below the unseeable horizon. It was the moment of maximum altitude, 1,462 feet, twelve seconds past "Happy New Year."

It is possible that Kukar remembered the bird strike of the day before, and he may have wondered if his controls had quit working. He kicked the rudder pedals once, hard, as if to check the response, although in an airplane the rudder is not normally used to get into a turn and cannot be used to get out of one. Kukar was flailing. Evidently he thought the airplane was still banked to the right, because he continued to steer and roll hard to the left.

If people on the shore noticed a falling comet, the passengers aboard the airplane probably noticed nothing at all. They sat easily in their seats and felt none of the heaviness of a well-flown turn as the Boeing, dropping its nose in perfect 1.0 G synchronization, rolled past knife-edge flight, and began to turn upside down. If the passengers had looked outside and behind, they would have seen a lit-up Bombay turning silently on its side and then floating above them like some strange city in the sky. They might have noticed the lack of feeling where feeling should be. Just then they could have poured themselves drinks without spilling a drop. For all the good it did them to remain seated, they could have stood up and danced the length of the inverted aisles.

That lack of feeling was of course precisely the problem for Kukar and his crew. The airplane was expressing a perfect spiral dive. Simulator studies at Boeing later showed that this moment, when it first rolled inverted to the left, was the pilots' last chance for recovery. If they had rolled fast to the right to level the wings and had aggressively raised the nose, subjecting the airplane to 2.5 Gs, they could have pulled out of the dive about 100 feet over the ocean. But that would have required them to know which way to turn.

In his blindness, Kukar did swing the control wheel hard to the right, and the airplane wobbled back to a ninety-degree bank.

The copilot repeated, "Mine has also toppled!"

The flight engineer may have leaned forward to point at the third, standby horizon. He said, "No, but go by this, Captain!"

But Kukar was still confused. He swung the control

wheel back to the left, and again the airplane rolled inverted. Seventeen seconds into the upset, the nose had dropped twenty-two degrees below the horizon. Though the airplane was still 1,100 feet above the water, its descent rate was shooting past 10,000 feet per minute, and before the end would reach three times that.

Only four seconds remained. Kukar said, "Just check the instrument! *Yar!*"

The copilot asked desperately, "Check what—" and was answered by the impact.

In the course of its spiral dive, Air India's Flight 855 had turned from west to south. It hit the water doing 380 miles per hour, with its nose pitched thirty-five degrees down and its wings banked inverted, eighteen degrees past the vertical. Kukar remained confused to the end and died steering left.

THE INDIAN GOVERNMENT convened a court of inquiry to establish an official cause for the accident. The hearings lasted several months. They took place in the heart of Bombay, in a sweltering courtroom whose latticework walls let in the dust and noise of the street outside. Pedestrians peered in through the openings. The inquiry was presided over by Justice M. N. Chandurkar, of Bombay's High Court, who had no previous experience in this area. A clerk recorded the testimony by pounding on an antique manual typewriter loaded with carbons. Flight 855's instruments had been shattered and dispersed by the impact, so the case was complicated by a lack of good physical evidence. Chandurkar, however, turned out to be an effective and intelligent questioner, unintimidated by the technical complexities of the case and unwilling to brook the double-talk of the interested parties—Air India, the pilots' union, Boeing, and their various expert witnesses, along with a slew of American attorneys who had converged anxiously on Bombay to monitor the proceedings. Chandurkar sorted through the conflicting testimonies with a fairness and certainty that ultimately won over all but the most partisan of the observers. The final report, written by Chandurkar himself, still stands as a quiet and credible piece of work, the expression of an almost naïve belief in the possibility of truth—this in contrast to the cynical rewriting of the story that took place later.

Chandurkar's first conclusion was simply that Kukar's artificial horizon had failed. During the hearing, expert witnesses had advanced three theories about such a failure. The first was that the instrument had frozen during the gentle right bank and had never moved again. The second was that the failure was "ratcheted," meaning that the instrument had responded normally to right rolls but had jammed whenever the airplane had rolled to the left. The third and most likely was that the instrument had not stuck at all but had failed by showing a steady and fictitious roll to the right, to which Kukar had slavishly responded by rolling to the left. Chandurkar did not try to decide among the three but reduced them to the essential: Kukar had rolled left and had died while trying to fly an indication that had gone bad.

Which raised the question of the warnings. The best artificial horizons, such as those on the 747, constantly test themselves; and when they detect a problem they drop a red warning "flag" across the face of the display. If such a flag had dropped, Kukar would certainly have seen it, and would have known to switch his focus immediately to the small standby horizon, or to hand over control of the airplane to the copilot. The airplane would hardly have wobbled. But as all pilots know, the flags themselves fail, and such failures, of safety systems generally, are especially dangerous because of the trust invested in them.

It was never Chandurkar's intention to absolve Kukar, and in the end he did not. At the same time, however, maybe because of his lack of previous involvement with the flying business, he was determined to describe the crisis in the cockpit not as others insisted it should have been but as he himself believed it was. After uncovering cases of flag failures in other 747s, he concluded that Kukar's instrument had deceived him twice over.

Chandurkar then went farther. The Air India cockpit was equipped with another safety device called a "comparator," which continuously compared the flight attitudes shown on the pilot and copilot artificial horizons and in the case of a disagreement between the two flashed a light on the master warning panel. Chandurkar agreed with the manufacturers that the comparator must have functioned correctly and that in the dimness of the cockpit the warning light must have been visible. But he pointed out that the warning had obviously been of no use to the pilots anyway, and he questioned the value of such a device in this particular case, when survival depended on the immediate interpretation of the panel's main instruments.

Chandurkar had glimpsed an especially modern aspect of our life inside the sky, and something that flight crews themselves need clearly to understand—that the cockpit's automated warnings, horns, and flashing lights provide largely just the appearance of safety and that for a variety of practical reasons no amount of automation can yet relieve pilots of the old-fashioned need to concentrate and think clearly in times of trouble.

Having examined the failures of the instruments, Chandurkar turned his attention to those of Kukar, who may once have been a good pilot but who at the time of the accident clearly was not.

"*Arey Yar!* My instrument!"

There it was on tape. Kukar had suspected a failure of his artificial horizon in plenty of time to keep the airplane under control if only he had been able to convince himself of it. If this lack of conviction seems hard to understand, remember that in the complete blackness of that night, a toppling artificial horizon line would have looked level to Kukar as he, in equal reaction, toppled the airplane to follow it. As an experienced airman, he seems to have noticed a bewildering discrepancy between his hard left steering and the lack of normal response on the face of his instrument. "*Arey Yar!*" Such a disconnection would have given him an intuitive perception of trouble, perhaps of control failure, and would explain his single exploratory kick of the rudder. A momentary confusion was inevitable. The sadness is that he sustained his confusion when directly in front of him a host of secondary instruments in a little stampeding herd clearly showed that the airplane was turning to the left, diving, and gaining speed. Kukar ignored them all. He had fixated on his artificial horizon, and in the urgency of the moment he could not summon the discipline to look away from it. His visual incapacitation is the most frustrating part of the story. He flew as if shackled to a single indication of the turn.

As the captain of the flight, Kukar was to blame for his copilot's errors as well. Pilots communicate with each other in unspoken ways, by the way they slouch in their seats, or throw the overhead switches, or handle the controls of the airplane in flight. The airlines fight back with standardized procedures and try to encourage enlightened regimes of teamwork and safe behavior. Nonetheless, the cockpit is like a club, and in the privacy of flight the sloppiness of a senior pilot will encourage the same attitude in his subordinates.

Kukar's copilot must have noticed what the airplane's "black boxes" later indicated—that Kukar made sloppy and unnecessary control motions on the runway, that he lifted off the pavement late and fast, that he rushed the flap retractions, that he climbed at too flat an angle, and that he started the right turn 500 feet below the altitude called for by the departure procedure. Less experienced pilots would not have made such mistakes. Kukar had proved capable of greater precision during his periodic flight checks, and he would no doubt have disapproved of such flying among his juniors, but he may also have felt that his improvisations were the prerogatives of a high-time pilot. And in the immediate sense he was right, too: Nothing he did during that takeoff was unsafe. But on the basis of his subsequent performance, his looseness now seems to indicate that he had grown careless. And to make matters worse, his copilot clearly did not think less of him for it.

Relaxing in the right seat, the copilot did not even bother to monitor the flight. When he heard Kukar's "My instrument!" he looked down at his own artificial horizon, expecting to see it showing the standard right turn, and was shocked to find it showing something quite the opposite—a nearly vertical bank to the left. Feeling nothing of that turn, checking none of the other instruments, he declared like some early airmail pilot that his indication was in error.

His stuttering "My . . . Mine's . . . Mine's is also toppled!" was not what Kukar needed to hear, and it marked the actual point—no matter what the simulator later showed—from which no recovery was possible.

The confusion was now absolute. Kukar said, "Check your instrument!" But against what? The circumstance that causes the spiral is the very circumstance that prevents its solution—in this case the collapse not just of one gyroscopic instrument but of the two pilots who refused to cross-check all the others.

From his position in the back of the cockpit, the flight engineer had the largest view of the instrument panel and therefore in this case the most accurate. The last seconds must have been frightening to him. The passengers and flight attendants knew nothing of the dive and had their lives extinguished so mercifully that they will in some sense forever be flying to Dubai. The pilots knew something, but not what, and they were fully occupied with their confusion. Only the flight engineer clearly saw the errors being made. It was not a nightmare, though that possibility must have crossed his mind. After so many years during which these things had happened only to others, he was the one now actually going down, out of control, crashing. There was no reason for this, and it didn't feel wild, but the instruments told an undeniable story. And yet he could do nothing but point.

"No, but go by this, Captain!"

Kukar did not even answer him. It is impossible to know what denials he was engaged in. Pilots train in simulators to handle all sorts of failures, sometimes heaped one on top of the other. But even the best of the simulators require a suspension of belief that never quite overcomes the understanding that they are pretend airplanes built for the purpose of experiencing failures and that no matter how poorly the pilots perform they will walk away unscathed. That, of course, is not true of failures inside the sky, where the first challenge is to suspend *disbelief* and where the urgency is real.

In any case the flight engineer's advice came too late. I refuse to turn away from the thought that the airplane's lights illuminated the ocean's surface at the last instant, that the surface appeared to surge at the airplane from somewhere above, and that the flight engineer flinched as the water exploded through the cockpit. It does not help to be polite about these details. The tangible consequence of any serious failure in flight can be just such an unstoppable insider's view.

CHANDURKAR WAS appropriately severe in his final judgment. He placed responsibility for the 213 deaths squarely upon Kukar and blamed the tragedy entirely on his inability, in a cockpit full of functioning instruments, to handle the failure of just one gyroscope. He wasted no emotion blaming the instrument itself, since it was obvious to him that even the best equipment can fail, which is one reason why pilots are needed. Instead, he recommended changes to Air India's recurrent training program and a renewed emphasis not only on the basics of instrument flying but also on the principles of communication within the cockpit. It all made perfect sense.

Nonetheless, Boeing was unhappy with Chandurkar's work—and for good reason. Armed with the official finding of an instrument failure, the families of the victims hired a New York law firm to bring suit in the United States against Boeing and the instrument manufacturers. The plaintiffs contended not only that the artificial horizon had caused the accident but that the comparator had failed as well, and furthermore that the designers of both devices had been negligent.

After years of maneuvering, the arguments were finally

presented in a federal court in Seattle, at the heart of Boeing country. They were heard in 1985, in a proceeding without a jury, by a judge named Fitzgerald. The first problem for Boeing and its codefendants was to persuade him that the artificial horizon and comparator had been well designed. This was not difficult. For every criticism of the designs made by the plaintiffs, Boeing had a credible answer. It so happened that Fitzgerald had been a pilot, and he understood the compromises—lightness, reliability, size—necessary in the practical world of flight. He must also have understood, given Boeing's reputation, that this was simply the best technology that money could buy. When Boeing asked the plaintiffs' experts to describe better designs, they could not. Fitzgerald decided against all claims of negligence.

Boeing's attorneys had a more difficult problem in attempting to maintain that Chandurkar's findings were wrong—that Air India's artificial horizon had indeed never failed. A more likely explanation, they said, was that Kukar had succumbed to vertigo. This goes back to William Ocker's discovery on the spinning Barany chair—that the sense of balance is worse than neutral in flight. A half-century later, while flying an airplane that Ocker could not have imagined, Kukar was overcome by a false sense of turning right, and he rolled left in response to it. His "My instrument!" was an expression of his primitive disbelief. His artificial horizon showed the same extreme left bank as the copilot's. The copilot's "Mine's is also toppled!" was evidence that he had looked across the panel and had seen that the instruments agreed. The comparator had worked perfectly because it had never illuminated. The flight engineer's recommendation of the standby horizon, "No, but go by this!" was meant as good advice on what to do when in doubt.

Chandurkar had heard these arguments in Bombay and had found them unconvincing, but Boeing's attorneys had now had years to refine them. To the question of how an experienced pilot could succumb to vertigo, they asked the equally difficult question of how such a pilot could succumb to a simple instrument failure.

Then they went after Kukar. He was an easy target—a heavy drinker and a diabetic who had temporarily lost his pilot's license for medical reasons three years before the accident. This too had been known to Chandurkar and dismissed as unimportant, but Boeing's attorneys had dug up additional dirt.

On New Year's Eve, the night before the accident, Kukar had gone out drinking with his family. Boeing found a retired filmmaker named Saran who lived in Kukar's Bombay apartment building and who while riding the elevator with him on New Year's morning had noticed that Kukar was in a particularly friendly mood, and that he smelled of alcohol.

Saran was a thin and ascetic man, a strict vegetarian, and for good reason something of an anti-American. It turned out that his son had been murdered while visiting Texas, and Saran held a grudge. He had no desire to help Boeing and the American insurance industry defend themselves against the families of the Indian dead. Nonetheless he was also a moralist, and because he did not approve of Kukar's intemperance, he allowed himself finally to be flown to Seattle for a deposition, which was recorded on video.

The camera focused tightly on Saran's face, creating the suspicion of a halo around his head. Saran told his story of smelling Kukar's breath.

Off camera, a voice asked aggressively, "How can you be sure you weren't smelling shaving lotion?"

Another voice said sarcastically, "Ah yes, the famous shaving lotion defense!"

In astonishment, Saran raised his hands to his mouth and said, "Do you mean he drank shaving lotion?"

When Judge Fitzgerald saw the video during the hearings he smiled for the only time.

No one claimed that Kukar was drunk when he got to the airport. But Boeing discovered that he was fasting and taking an oral hypoglycemic in order to fool a glucose tolerance test that he was scheduled to take the following week. The combination of the drug, the fasting, and the drinking of the night before meant that when Kukar taxied out for takeoff he was suffering from low blood sugar—a dangerous condition for a diabetic, and potentially disturbing to the functioning of the inner ear.

That was Boeing's pitch. Kukar was an experienced pilot but also a diabetic with a dangerous sense of balance. The sloppiness of his takeoff and departure fit the profile of someone who already was suffering from vertigo and ignoring his instruments. After he crossed the shoreline and no longer had a visible horizon, he inevitably lost control. And his copilot was simply incompetent.

The same medical evidence could have been used to explain why, after the failure of his artificial horizon, Kukar was unable to cope. Even so, Fitzgerald accepted Boeing's scenario and declared in the end that no failure of the instrument had occurred. It is hard to know whether he really believed this or whether perhaps he was engaged instead in a deeper, airman's understanding of justice. When later I asked the plaintiffs' attorney about it, he called the decision terrible. On the narrow question of the instrument's failure, he was probably right. Boeing's attorney disagreed, and called the decision wise. And in a larger sense than he intended, he was right. The killing was all Kukar's fault anyway.

In the final analysis, the underlying cause seems oddly enough to have been the very extent of Kukar's flying experience. Although this is difficult for outsiders to comprehend, there comes a point in a pilot's life when the sky feels like home. In my case it came after 4,000 flight hours, during a certain takeoff on a bright winter morning in Lincoln, Nebraska, westbound to California. Once airborne I retracted the landing gear and rolled into an early left turn, and as I looked back at the leading edge of the wing slicing stiffly above the frozen prairie, I realized that no difference existed for me between the earth and sky; it was as if with these wings I could now walk in the air.

Kukar too must have known such a moment and may have fallen into the trap which in later years can lie beyond it—a frustration with the complexities of life on the ground, and a lack of control in personal affairs heightened by love affairs or drink or failing health, which defeats old pilots and leads them to the tragic conclusion that they have ever only been truly at home when seated in their obedient airplanes in the sky.

Yes, the sky at times can seem as familiar as a familiar landscape, but on dark nights and inside the clouds its alien nature reemerges. Again then it becomes a surreal and dangerous place across which we humans may move, but only with care and wonder. The cockpit at such times is like a capsule hurtling through some distant reach of space. And yet that reach of space may lie just overhead, and may be entered only seconds after an airplane lifts off the runway. Pilots going out into those conditions need to hesitate before they power up for their takeoffs. They need that moment to run through the first critical moves of the flight, to shift their thoughts away from the ground, and to summon the concentration necessary to navigate the strange sky ahead. Kukar did none of that. He flew badly and crashed because he leaped too willingly into what even for him remained the unknown.

FIVE

Inside an Angry Sky

THE FIRST WINTER of my cargo flying was the worst because my days spent writing seemed increasingly wasteful, and I had yet to understand my nights. As others sat down to their warm dinners, I headed out alone and in darkness from the San Francisco airport, on routes across all the mountainous West, through a steady succession of weather fronts and violent low-pressure systems spinning in from the North Pacific. It was dangerous, low-paid work, in battered old airplanes that were poorly maintained by mechanics who joked about "pencil whipping" the equipment into the air. It taught me hard lessons about in-flight failures—of engines, electrical systems, and instruments. More important, it taught me about the cockpit as a monastic cell—to hold myself in it at the head of rain-soaked runways under heavy clouds, and to reduce the instrument panel to its barest indications, and only then to push the throttles forward and allow the wings to lift me into the storms and the inner landscapes of the mind.

It was during that difficult winter that I reread *Night Flight,* Antoine de Saint-Exupéry's classic romanticization of self-sacrifice among the pioneering French airmail pilots in South America. Although Saint-Exupéry was one of those early pilots, he was a notoriously dreamy one; and it was as a working pilot myself now that I rejected his work as inauthentic, disdaining its sense of the common good, its maudlin emotionalism, and its overwrought musings on the glories of the mission. Closer to my own emotions then was another old novel, *The Death Ship,* written by the German anarchist B. Traven, which I stumbled across in paperback at the airport newsstand in El Paso among the usual cowboy stories and religious tracts. Presented as a sea adventure "by the author of *The Treasure of Sierra Madre!*" with a cover drawing of men swimming away from a sinking ship, it was in fact a bitter political manifesto written in a false proletarian voice, the story of a doomed and nationless stoker who cursed the society that excluded him and the commerce that sent him to sea. I myself had nothing to be bitter about—I had chosen this path—but I was cold and tired and underpaid, and I could not help resenting my cargos of last-minute gifts and unimportant documents, the casual spinoffs of smarter or more certain lives than mine. That winter threatened never to end.

And then one dark night, while strapped into a cockpit spitting snow, I crossed a cloud crevasse and glimpsed the lights of a single ranch house far below. Despite my earlier disdain, a scene from Saint-Exupéry came to mind. I have read the words again since.

Sometimes, after a hundred miles of steppes as desolate as the sea, he encountered a lonely farmhouse that seemed to be sailing backwards from him in a great prairie sea, with its freight of human lives.

My airplane was running poorly, and shuddering at times as though it might shake itself apart, and staggering under a load of ice that had accumulated along its leading edges because its deicing system had once again failed, but it was the view of those lights that unnerved me.

Gathered round their lamp-lit table, those peasants do not guess that their desire carries so far, out into the vastness of the night that hems them in.

The depth of the clouds, fleetingly apparent through the crevasse, forced on me the realization of an unbridgeable distance from the world. Saint-Exupéry had after all known something about this night sky. Like one of his imagined characters, I began actively to contemplate the possibility that I would never return from it—something that previously I had believed no real pilot would take the time to do.

I told myself that I was just discouraged. But for weeks afterward I could not shake the sense of doom. The weather did not relent. Every evening I drove in isolation to the airport, away from the satisfied city crowds, away from friendships and the beauty of women, to endure the delays for takeoff under black rain, when sometimes a terrible sleepiness would overcome me. Saint-Exupéry knew that sleepiness, too; he called it an inertia which paralyzes men who face the unknown. To me it felt like complete physical relaxation, anticipation, the slowest form of fear. A more active fear took its place after takeoff, causing me to fly slavishly, without raising my eyes from the instruments. It was dangerous because I kept yearning for the ground.

The winter closed with a violent storm that flooded the rivers and blew down power lines and trees. The sheer force of that storm forced me at last to look up from the instruments again—and when I did I discovered a place fantastic even to me, far away in the wild winds, where rain fell upward and blizzards blew among cloud mountains and the walls of great caverns erupted in light. The passage of my flight through that weather attracted an electrical charge from the clouds, a flash and bang that burned a hole in the right engine nacelle and mushroomed the top of the tail—and the airplane just shrugged it off. After returning I stood in the wind-driven rain and watched the workers back their vans up to the airplane to unload its cargo. I did not tell them where I had been. How could they have understood? Even to me it was a wonder that this little metal machine, so battered and unloved, had carried me there. It was late at night, and I should have driven home and slept, but I was not tired. I felt renewed not because I had survived but because I had the means and the inclination to fly again into that angry sky. No pilot could ever be at home there, but I for one had stopped yearning for the ground.

THAT LITTLE PIECE of history may explain why, years later, I sometimes still go out hunting for bad weather, flying low in simple airplanes to explore the inner reaches of the clouds. Less experienced pilots occasionally join me, not to learn formal lessons about weather flying but with a more advanced purpose in mind—to accompany me in the slow accumulation of experience through circumstances that never repeat in a place that defies mastery. Our destinations lie in the turbulent eddies of the lower atmosphere, places called "cyclones" or "lows" on the weather maps, but also known simply as "storms," a word which better reflects their effect on the sky.

It is obvious that flying intentionally into such places, and lingering there, is the kind of behavior easily disapproved of. We have critics for whom the intentional pursuit of severe weather amounts to heresy; they grow angry about the risks we take, and about our apparent lack of judgment. I have always understood their concern. But the pursuit of such weather is an internal act, not a public one, and it is neither as reckless nor as arbitrary as at first it may seem. It involves dangers, of course, but to a degree unimaginable to the critics, those dangers are controllable. Because of the mental concentration required by such flying, there is never the slightest question of survival—in fact, it is such discipline that gives the exercise its content.

The secret of good storm flying is to stay low, in slow
and vulnerable airplanes, and to resist the pursuit of performance. By the standards of practical transportation,
therefore, it is an artificial problem. Most weather lies
within the first 20,000 feet of the ground, where gravity
compresses the atmospheric mass into a dense soup, and
above which the airlines for economic reasons as well as
safety and comfort must climb and cruise. Engineers have
designed away the storms, leaving professional pilots to fret
about the kind of unimportant turbulence that startles
their most anxious passengers. It seems a pity. With a few
simple equations, meteorologists can prove that the lower
atmosphere, where the simple airplane must fly, remains
rich with surprise.

That is the allure of storm flying. There is no graduation
from the experience, only an end to each flight. The tech-
niques we practice involve a certain calmness under pressure. More important, they involve ways of picturing the
storms, of understanding the weather from the weather's
inside. The airplane is merely our tool. We ride it aloft,
descend in it to refuel or sleep, then ride it again, mixing nights into days, listening to the changing accents of
air traffic control, exploring a continent that lies entirely
within the sky. We fly the forecast, turn, and probe the
forecast's flaws. But we are not theoreticians. The airplane's
forward motion imposes a crude immediacy on our
thoughts, so that even when we do not understand the
weather, we may pretend that we do. Flying as much as
writing teaches the need for such fictions, for discerning
the patterns in a disorderly world.

On a recent Christmas, for instance, a storm was born above the Pacific in a place which for most of us can exist only in the imagination. Picture an air-world of mountains and valleys through which strong eastward winds meander. The air is a gas, and like other gasses it is compressible, and has weight, and is subject to the simple physics of motion. The winds are air molecules driven by the sun's heat and steered on a global scale by the earth's rotation. The mountains and valleys through which they move are immense. They consist of semi-permanent "highs" into which, strangely, the winds descend, and "lows" into which the winds climb. The explanation for this apparently peculiar behavior lies entirely in the language: The terms "high" and "low" refer not to altitude but to pressure, variations caused by the sun's unequal heating of the earth's surface. When the molecules are cooled, they compress downward into a "high," and when they are warmed, they expand upward into a "low." These pressure variations constitute the sky's elemental topography.

Now imagine something equally elemental, an atmospheric war caused by the same solar inequality. Across the Pacific theater, past China and Siberia to Canada, lies a great front, an undulating zone of conflict between jealous masses of polar and tropical air. The front shifts with the seasons but endures year after year. It is accompanied by high-altitude winds that have been squeezed and accelerated into a jet stream flowing at speeds over 100 miles per hour. Swooping and swerving among the contours of the sky, the jet stream serves as a powerful catalyst. East of the

Aleutians, it catches a high-altitude corner of the North Pacific's largest permanent low, in a part of the sky where already the atmosphere is unsettled. The immediate effect is a further drop in air pressure as molecules begin to scatter more quickly than they can be replaced. Such high-altitude scattering, known to meteorologists as "horizontal divergence," is the most important mechanism in the life of storms. It creates a form of hunger whereby a pocket of low-pressure air sucks at the denser air immediately below.

That is what happened that Christmas. The storm's birth was typically fast. Cooling as it rose, the Pacific air condensed into cloud and worked up an appetite of its own. The pressure continued to drop. The result was an odd sort of digging at the sky—the creation of an atmospheric hole through which the air surged upward, away from the earth. The hole steepened as it deepened, the upward surge intensified, and rain began to fall. Satellites photographed it on the second day. From across the horizons, low-altitude winds rushed forward, only to be deflected to the right by the globe's rotation. The deflected winds gave the storm its counterclockwise twirl and an indication of its power. Inexorably it drew the opposing air masses into direct conflict. Steered by steadier winds aloft, the storm drifted eastward toward the continent like an eddy spinning downstream. By the third day it appeared on the map as a massive winter storm, centered 500 miles west of the Alaskan panhandle, sending the long arm of a cold front toward the California coast, where I waited with two other pilots.

Our airplane was a single-engine Bonanza, a weather-scarred veteran that we had used before. The plan was for the two less-experienced pilots to swap legs—for each to fly in turn as the other observed from the back seat—and for me to remain up front throughout. We gave ourselves a week. On the eve of the departure, we discussed where to meet the storm. It was due to hit the West Coast by morning, bringing low cloud, rain, and snow from Vancouver to San Francisco.

We considered flying north to Seattle, toward the storm's center, where even after its passage the weather might linger. Seattle is famously good for cloud. It also offers the upslope of the Cascade Mountains, where we were likely now to be blocked by heavy icing—a deadly condition into which our airplane was not equipped to fly. The challenge for us would to find a way *around* such conditions, rather than through them. Moreover, the same Cascade upslope threatened to wring the wetness from the storm, leaving it to cross the western deserts in a dry and weakened form. The deserts are deserts for a reason. By flying to Seattle we might put ourselves into a corner of the continent, and after a day finish with no weather at all. The forecasts seemed uncertain. So we decided to leave the storm temporarily behind and spend the first day jumping east to Kansas City, where a smaller disturbance had stirred the clouds. There, we would reassess the map. The forecasts seemed contradictory and uncertain. We had to trust that the storm would survive its mountain crossings, reassemble, and catch up with us in a more difficult form.

At 200 miles per hour, the flight from San Francisco to Kansas City took all day. We climbed out of northern California through the storm's bands of rain and cloud and, in search of tail winds, headed into the warm and clear skies of the Southwest. We refueled in Winslow, Arizona. Toward evening, as we crossed the Rockies, we checked by radio and found that Kansas City was reporting lowering clouds and snow, an unexpected downturn to threaten our arrival. It seemed possible now that the weather would continue to worsen and, because of ice and low ceilings, block the flight during its final stage, when our choices would be limited by lack of fuel.

We kept going but discussed an escape plan that would allow us to retreat even from retreat. Such planning is a large part of storm flying. Airplanes give pilots plenty of time to consider possible trouble, but when the trouble hits, it hits fast. Retreat then means climbing, descending, turning, or slowing to save fuel. Preparing those moves in advance—and preparing for their failure—involves a layered logic that is not difficult to understand, but it also requires that pilots confront their worst fears. Unfocused anxiety is the emotion people must avoid. Circumstances in the atmosphere combine to kill the wishful or the distracted.

After dark at 11,000 feet over Kansas we hit the weather, which opened like jaws above and below, then closed firmly around us. The clouds on the inside were pitch black. The engine sounded rough only to the imagination. The instruments glowed reassuringly in soft yellow light. The outside observer would have noticed little action: three ordinary Americans dressed in ordinary clothes, watching nearly motionless dials, talking in half-sentences about the flight, talking about politics, occasionally transmitting to air traffic control. We flew on into the night, took a frosting during the descent, broke free of the clouds about a mile from the runway on final approach, and landed with plenty of fuel in the tanks. In downtown Kansas City, where we slept, steam rose from the manhole covers. The streets looked abandoned to an Arctic winter.

Spring blew in overnight. Already by breakfast, under leaden clouds, the temperature had climbed to forty degrees, and Missourians were talking about mud. The tone was apocalyptic, as it often is when people wake up to the weather. A bookish waiter at the hotel blamed global warming. Out at the airport, the Christian pumping fuel mentioned trouble in the Middle East.

Our own interests were more immediate. Shepherded by upper winds, the Pacific storm had barely endured the climb across the mountains and had emerged onto the Wyoming plains in a mechanically weakened condition. Once there, however, it reformed and gathered strength on the southern flank of a great dome of cold Canadian air that was spanning the continent. Spinning purposefully again, the storm attached itself to that boundary—the line where the cold air met the warmer air to its south—and drifted eastward, chewing deeply into its air-mass hosts. On the scale of a continent, the map was clear. The air-mass boundary formed a single deeply curving front that

extended for nearly 2,000 miles across the American heart-
land, from Wyoming to upstate New York. The storm
swirled like a cataclysmic whirlpool along that line. To
the west of its center, the counterclockwise circulation had
swept the Canadian air mass far to the south, bringing cold
temperatures to Salt Lake City and Las Vegas. Here in
Kansas City, to the east of the center, the same whirlpool
circulation had generated a powerful southerly flow, forcing the winter temporarily from the streets. In other words,
our gamble had paid off. The unusually warm weather in
Missouri meant that a big disruption was under way.

The official weather briefing sounded shrill. The storm
center was moving fast and was expected to cross the Mississippi by afternoon. Already the worst weather lay to the
northeast, where the warm air aloft was overriding cold
air close to the ground. We heard reports of moderate
and severe turbulence, ice, and snow falling hard across
the Great Lakes. The shadow of Lake Michigan promised
near-blizzard conditions. Huddled over our maps, we prepared to fly into it with a 500-mile run to South Bend,
Indiana. The ground rules were clear: Safety would lie in
the ready retreat, but success would depend on our determination and mental flexibility. Storm flying in such an
airplane is more a negotiation than a brawl. You slip
through a few miles at a time, judging and probing the
clouds, moving higher or lower, turning, detouring, rarely
surrendering. That was all we could be sure of in advance.
On the intimate scale of an airplane, the weather promises
eternal complexity.

We took off over the downtown and climbed into warm gray clouds. Moisture rolled up the windshield and became a tapping rain. The weather held clouds within the clouds, with textures and discernible edges. We rode the storm easily at first. At 9,000 feet, where we leveled, the temperature held a few degrees above freezing. Occasionally we emerged into cloud chambers with floors and ceilings joined by misty columns. They must have been beautiful. Maybe they were even interesting. But an airplane does not allow for an uninvolved appreciation of the weather. For the moment we had two specific concerns—the possibility of dangerous icing at our altitude ahead, and the certainty of it already directly below. Shuddering through light turbulence, shoved by the winds, we approached the Mississippi and asked for updates on the winter now enduring beneath us. Moline, Illinois, reported low clouds, snow, and a surface temperature of only thirteen degrees. In the worst case now, retreat might require a slow run against head winds all the way back to Kansas City. The forecast called for freezing temperatures to return there by afternoon. If they returned sooner, even that retreat could be cut off.

Pilots are forever being pestered with platitudes, including that which advises them to know their limitations in order to stop short of them. But there is no reason to enter into storm flying only to give ground. And there is also such a thing as being too careful. If you give in to your fears, if you don't push gently against them, you will turn around too soon. And the next time you fly, you will turn around sooner. Eventually you will turn around before takeoff, which is the unhappy fate of some pilots: to choose finally never to fly again.

So past the Mississippi, when we ran out of warm air, we accepted the risk and kept going. The air temperature dropped through freezing, and our wings began to ice over dangerously. Hoping only for a temporary reprieve—an increase of merely two degrees would have melted the ice—we descended to 7,000 feet and found clear air between cloud layers. Without the clouds' sustaining moisture, the wing ice slowly evaporated. Once again, an outside observer would have noticed little. We watched the instruments. We made a mental concession to the weather and stopped anticipating our arrival in South Bend. It was too far ahead to matter. Deep inside the storm, we worked mile by mile.

The temperatures aloft continued to fall, just as the barometric pressure rose. A meteorologist would say we had passed north of the volatile air-mass boundary, into a dome of Arctic air. But seen from within, there wasn't much change; the weather remained thick with cloud. Icing occasionally, maneuvering to stay between the layers, climbing once to 13,000 feet, we continued for another hour. Snow blew in through the ventilators. Somewhere over central Illinois the clouds opened for a few miles and we glimpsed a frozen strip mine, a high school, and fields colored the same whitish gray as the sky.

Chicago passed in the chattering of air traffic control. By the time the cloud layers merged, the temperature had dropped to minus five degrees, and the clouds consisted of frozen crystals that bounced harmlessly off the wings. We had won a temporary victory over the ice and could plan again for South Bend. The airport there was equipped with a standard instrument approach, a radio beam we could follow to a point 200 feet above the ground and a half-mile short of the runway. From there, we would have to see the runway to land. On the basis of the reported weather, we expected to. The South Bend approach controller greeted us as we drew near and he watched us on radar as we flew a fast descent and shot the approach. We landed in falling and blowing snow. We intended to refuel, talk through the flight, and set out again in the afternoon. The temperature registered ten degrees as we taxied slowly in. No one emerged from the hangars. We found the ground crew inside watching football. They looked up at us blankly, as if they could not imagine where we had come from. Had they asked, we would have answered, Kansas City.

MONTHS LATER, armed with old weather maps from our flight, I drove to the National Weather Service's Operations Center, in suburban Camp Springs, Maryland. The Operations Center is the collection point for weather observations nationwide. A staff meteorologist there, Paul Kocin, had agreed to go over the record of the flight with me and to make sense of my memories.

Kocin turned out to be an affable New Yorker in his thirties, neatly dressed in jeans and a checked shirt. He led me through humming rooms where banks of electronics monitored the mass of incoming observations and meteorologists worked in teams to meet the schedule of summaries, weather maps, and national-scale forecasts necessary for the regional offices. Giant TV screens flashed satellite sequences of a growing Gulf Coast storm, adding urgency to the day. At a special briefing, the sector chiefs reported in expressing concern about the storm's overnight movements. Despite the placidity of their expressions—they yawned and slouched and doodled—it was clear to me that the meteorologists there felt a certain thrill at working on the front edge of time.

Kocin's duties included supervising the three-hour surface analysis chart, the basic weather map from which most of the nation's forecasts are derived. He led me to a large horizontal screen on which an electronic outline of the United States was filled with symbols representing the latest weather observations.

Rhetorically Kocin asked, "What's going on here?"

He answered himself, "I have no idea."

Nonetheless, after peering at the electronic chart for a few minutes, he used a pointing device to take the indication of a cold front from Arkansas and casually stretch it eastward. He said, "I don't even really know what I'm looking for. I hope it'll become obvious."

He said that experience still plays an important role in weather work, and to show me what he meant, he pivoted to look at the satellite and radar displays. "Is there a squall line there? Yeah, sure is. A good one."

As a result, he rearranged the map again, hooked the

front through Nashville, and zoomed in on Ohio to study wind and pressure changes there. This sort of redefinition of the weather lasted an hour. I sat on a high upholstered stool and watched—my government in action, producing an orderly and convincing view of the sky. I sipped coffee. The operations room felt as comfortable and secure as a command bunker. It amused me to give no thought to the pilots out there in the confusion of the real world.

The next day, over a sandwich in the lunchroom, Kocin confided, "People around here know this about me. I try to keep it from my outside friends. It's not so bad anymore, but I used to be a real weather-weenie."

Politely, I acted surprised. "What do you mean?"

"You know, in high school I started keeping temperature and pressure logs."

I nodded sympathetically, because in recent years I myself had taken to reading *Weatherwise,* a magazine that promotes just such behavior.

Weatherwise is published in Washington, D.C., by a nonprofit foundation that rescues worthy periodicals. Its circulation has recently doubled to 13,000, largely due to the efforts of its young editors, the sort of fresh college graduates who take the job on a whim and discover only afterward their own fascination for the subject. They know how to satisfy their readers, offering up the earnestly informative essays the readers expect—on blocking highs, jet streams, and Doppler radars—but also digressing into the sort of surprising subjects that keep the magazine fresh. In a recent issue, for instance, they ran a cover story on the importance of "weather spying" in nineteenth-century

Central Asia, along with another piece on exciting careers in forensic meteorology—the plaintiff says she slipped, but was the driveway icy?

Weatherwise gets read cover to cover, then passed around. The letters to the editor are passionate. And the ads— for home weather stations, computer services, forecasting contests, conventions, and videos—are almost as interesting. "Watch *Camille* in action!" The ads hint at a large and closeted population of weather watchers.

Weatherwise writes up the action heroes. There are, for instance, the diehards who drive against the fleeing traffic, flash press credentials at the police, and head into the center of tropical hurricanes.

The electrical explosions across the city grew more intense, yet the fury of the wind swallowed up all the sound save the car alarms whining inside the garage. Eventually even the alarms were overwhelmed by the whistling wind. Around 4 AM all hell broke loose. I have experienced severe storms with winds in excess of 75 mph, but these gusts were blowing at well over 140 mph. . . . By now only an occasional thud—some building collapsing or losing a roof—would punctuate the noise. Windows from the surrounding buildings imploded, scattering glass everywhere. I looked down at my arm and saw blood, not knowing when I'd been cut. Putting on my reading glasses to protect my eyes, I made a mental note: next time, bring goggles.

And there is Professor T. T. Fujita, the hands-on "Mr. Tornado," who has devised a tornado scale based on destruction, from the mild F-0, which knocks over chimneys and billboards, to the full-blown F-5, which is the kind of twister that surprised Dorothy in *The Wizard of Oz:* "Winds greater than 261 mph. Incredible damage. Lifts strong frame houses off foundations, sweeps them away, and dashes them to pieces; debarks trees; badly damages steel-reinforced concrete structures."

Among hard-core weather watchers, tornadoes are known affectionately as "beasts" and are considered to have one clear advantage over hurricanes: Because they are localized, only hundreds of yards across, you can drive right up to them safely. During the spring spawning season, hundreds of hunters chase around the Great Plains, trying to capture one on videotape from up close. There are risks, of course. The F-4 will make projectiles, for instance, of full-sized rental cars. Nonetheless, the hunt has become so popular that at least one bad movie has been made about it, and a man in Norman, Oklahoma, calling himself Whirlwind Tours, has begun to offer two-week tornado safaris. His game hunters come from around the world.

Most weather watchers are less adventurous. They set their computers to quick-start onto the best new radar maps, and they monitor the Weather Channel with its excited sky-is-falling banter and its occasional live reports of genuine meteorological disaster. But they seem perfectly happy to stay home and measure the weather, second-guess the official forecasts, compare notes, and quarrel over weather records.

One of the *Weatherwise* editors, a young man who also had a passion for baseball statistics, put it this way to me: "Look, the weather is important. There is a strong feeling out there that you can't just let it pass by."

But "passing by" is precisely what the weather does.

This frustration is apparently what motivated the greatest living weather watcher, the weather historian David Ludlum, who in 1948 founded *Weatherwise*. Ludlum, who had earned a Princeton doctorate in conventional history, became an Army Air Corps meteorologist during World War II. For three weeks he delayed the crucial invasion of Cassino, Italy, until he could predict that the weather would be favorable. In thanks, the Army named the invasion "Operation Ludlum." And you can still see Ludlum playing himself in the 1953 Paramount production *From Cassino to Korea.*

No wonder he returned from the war convinced that weather could not be ignored in the writing of history. We know about the wind's defeat of the Spanish Armada and about Napoleon's difficulties with the climate in Russia, but just how hot and humid were the American colonies on July 4, 1776? And what did Lincoln *really* feel at Gettysburg? More generally, what about New England weather during the last decade of the last century? This was the sort of question that came to obsess Ludlum. He wrote books full of answers.

As a reader of his magazine, I came to the conclusion that an interest in disembodied weather history—in weather history for its own sake—is the surest sign of the genuine weather-weenie. Paul Kocin did not need to admit his past to me. I had already seen his book, *Snowstorms along the Northeastern Coast of the United States: 1955 to 1985*, and I understood his predicament: We live in a society that does not reward these efforts. Try discussing forgotten weather with strangers and watch their reactions. Pilots, too, will grow impatient. They navigate through history without the education to make sense of it. That is why I felt lucky to find Kocin: he was just the man to rescue my storm from its passing.

We spread the relevant weather maps on a conference table. Kocin started with a regret that my students and I had missed the more interesting conditions. It so happened that the day before our departure from San Francisco, a tightly wound low had left the Canadian plains and sailed fast to Alabama. Kocin called it an "Alberta Clipper" and said he remembered this particular one for its turbulent wake. And that was nothing compared to events of the following morning when, as we lifted off from the West Coast, a complex system of twin storms and connecting fronts formed on the other side of the nation. Research meteorologists are still sifting the data to explain what happened next.

That gray winter morning Kocin had just assumed his duties in the operations room when he noticed that the atmospheric pressure at a weather station in Georgia had dived sharply and climbed again. Kocin watched with growing excitement as the next station to the north reported the same phenomenon. The pressure drop was as catastrophic as a crash, and it seemed to be moving quickly up the Eastern seaboard.

Kocin faxed the first hastily scribbled alert to the regional forecasting centers: "Possible gravity wave!"

He got the warning out just in time. The wave sped into Pennsylvania and New England like the impulse of a whip. Cities reported incredible snowfall rates of up to six inches an hour. Weather enthusiasts rushed to their stations. Citizens were amazed to see lightning and to hear the snow thunder. Traffic snarled. Across the Northeast a million little invasions were delayed.

Our Pacific storm lacked that punch. Kocin worked diligently to help me understand its birth, but his attention kept drifting back to the pressure drop in the East. He truly regretted that we had missed it.

I did not have to remind Kocin that on that first day New England remained out of reach of our slow airplane. I wanted to keep the conversation focused on our storm, now in the Midwest. Kocin said he understood, but a little gulf had opened between us: Weather watchers are drawn to history's most violent weather, but pilots are drawn to the weather they have flown.

I tried to describe the conditions we had encountered on the flight from Kansas City to South Bend. Kocin listened politely but remained unimpressed. He had the advantage of trusting the weather map. This was hardly surprising. Theoreticians and practitioners will often disagree. And ordinary history usually looks more orderly from a distance than from up close. Kocin doubted, for instance, that we had found much bad weather in South Bend. He mentioned perhaps some trivial lake effect.

BUT THE WEATHER in South Bend seemed plenty bad to me. The storm was advancing fast and was now expected to slip eastward along the air-mass boundary and into Massachusetts by the next morning. We decided to cross the notorious Alleghenies and spend the night in Harrisburg, Pennsylvania. It would be a hard-fought flight most of the way there, but for the next day it would gain us maneuvering room over the coastal plain, with its low cruising altitudes and its frequent well-equipped airports. If everything went according to plan, the storm's center would pass over us while we slept. In the morning we would head for Boston and hit the weather again from the south.

In the meantime, the weather conditions had worsened in South Bend. Bundled against the cold winds sweeping the airport, we fueled and checked the airplane. By the time we taxied out, in late afternoon, the visibility had dropped to a third of a mile in heavy snow. In principle such visibility was less than we would need to see the runway at the end of an instrument approach should we encounter a problem after takeoff and need to return, though in a true emergency we felt we could in practice make it to the runway. Conditions ahead for 200 miles looked almost as low. The tops were expected to be at 22,000 feet, about our capabilities. The airlines were reporting moderate turbulence. The only good news was that the temperatures remained too cold, probably, for icing to threaten us.

We took off and were swallowed by cloud. The effect was immediate and dramatic—the ground vanished so quickly that it might never have existed. Indiana became an abstraction, South Bend an uncertain memory. The clouds were rough, but it was the psychological severity of this transition from the ground to the weather that made the airplane difficult to control. I asked the pilot beside me at the controls to stop throwing switches, to stop writing down frequencies and fuel settings, to stop listening to the Morse identifiers of the navigational stations, and please simply to concentrate on flying. A good pilot is one who knows when *not* to follow procedures.

The thin voice of air traffic control, with a woman's laughter in the background, offered a thread to the Midwest, but for us the world had been reduced again to the instrument panel. We were tired and did not talk. We were together, but also each of us was alone. The flight passed not by the minute or hour but, as flight often does, in a suspended condition of time, an abstraction of speed disconnected from progress across the surface of the earth. Harrisburg existed merely as the anticipation of a faraway descent through the clouds. There was nothing to do about it yet. We flew on in a meditative mood. The airplane ran strongly. The landscape that surrounded us was one of our own making.

Night came at 9,000 feet in continuing cloud and snow. Our forward lights bored horizontal holes into the blackness through which snowflakes rushed back at us in frenzied assaults. Out at the wing tips, the strobes caused the night to bloom. We did not exclaim over the beauty of this wilderness but recognized it as J. B. Jackson might have wished he could—as fully involved participants, judging our surroundings critically because the conditions remained rough and hostile.

Over eastern Ohio we broke suddenly into the clear air of an Arctic night. The lights of Cleveland lit the northern horizon. The air-mass boundary lay just to our south, in the black wall of cloud from which we had emerged. Paul Kocin would have been delighted with the view: The weather lay exactly where the map said it should. We sailed over Pittsburgh, which was still digging out from Kocin's gravity wave, and we hit the clouds again for the brief crossing of the Alleghenies and the high-speed descent into Harrisburg, where we landed on an icy runway. We were content then to let the storm center pass overhead.

In the morning we woke to a heavy snowfall outside the hotel windows and realized immediately that the weather had gone wrong. Rather than tracking as forecasted to New England, the storm had slowed over the Mississippi and had assumed a classic stance, extending a cold front southwest across Oklahoma and a stationary front eastward across the Virginias to the Chesapeake. Along the stationary front now, warm sluggish southern air was trying to climb the dense Arctic air that had packed at low altitude over the Northeast. Harrisburg lay in the thick of the resulting disturbance. The woman on the Weather Channel sounded tense and excited.

We got a ride to the airport and telephoned for a formal weather briefing. The ceiling and visibility were close to the minimum requirements of the instrument approach. And the temperature gradient looked ominous: On the ground it registered a normal twenty-one degrees, but rather than cooling further with altitude, it stayed about the same, just below freezing, to a point near the tops of the clouds. A DC-9 climbing out of Harrisburg reported heavy icing from the surface all the way to 16,000 feet— conditions too deep and dangerous for our unprotected wings. There would be no escape after a takeoff. The storm had grounded us. We settled by the hangar telephone and waited for a break.

Ice on any airplane is scary stuff. Allowed to accumulate, it disturbs the lifting air flow across the wings and tail and causes them finally to stop flying. When the wings stop flying, the airplane does one of two things: It descends into a flat, mushing, semi-controllable impact with the ground; or it shudders, drops its nose, maybe rolls, and hits the ground much harder. When the tail stops flying, the effect is even more dramatic: The airplane dives violently, irreversibly, and may gain so much speed that it breaks apart even before it hits the ground.

Other complications are possible. The American Eagle ATR turboprop that crashed at Roselawn, Indiana, in October 1994, was a new design with an unexpected vulnerability to ice, which under narrow circumstances caused the airplane to roll out of control. Immediately after the accident, pilots at the airline's Chicago base balked at continuing to fly that type of airplane into winter weather. The company answered with apparent concern, suggesting that the pilots seek psychological counseling. Pilots everywhere smiled bitterly. The fear of ice is a healthy and rational emotion.

Still, ice can become an obsession. Once you start looking for it you see it all around. Watch an airplane standing on the ground in sleet or freezing rain. Ice accumulates in glistening sheets across its top surfaces. Airport crews spray it off with an alcohol mixture before the airplane taxis. If there is a delay before takeoff and the ice comes back, the crews have to spray it off again. Some airliners have crashed because of the inconvenience of that second deicing, which may require a return to the ramp. The resulting delays are measured by the hour. In response, a few airports have installed taxi-through spray racks near the runways. Pilots need no counseling to use them.

Once an airplane takes off, the obsession changes. Now you see ice growing forward from the sharp leading edges—on the wings, tail, and engine nacelles. If the airplane is propeller-driven, you imagine it on the spinning blades, where it grows even faster. In-flight icing may come from sleet or freezing rain, but more commonly it comes from the super-cooled water particles that make up the clouds at temperatures between thirty-two and about fifteen degrees Fahrenheit. Super-cooled water particles are droplets floating in such perfect equilibrium that they maintain a liquid form in below-freezing air. Then along comes the below-freezing airplane. The disturbed droplets turn instantly to ice and stick to its leading edges. The effect is that of a telephone pole in an "ice fog." Only here the wind is blowing several hundred miles an hour. Because of the airplane's speed, the growth can be explosive and can lead to loss of control within just a few minutes. The critical load varies, but beyond perhaps three inches of ice, flight becomes a gamble. Airliners are protected by heated leading edges, or by rubber boots which inflate to knock off the load once it accumulates. Our airplane had no such devices. So we waited in Harrisburg.

By noon we had ruled out New England, where the conditions had started to duplicate our own, but the weather to our south was opening. Cloud bases at 2,500 feet were reported over Wilmington and Washington, D.C., and the surface temperature at Norfolk was an ice-melting forty-five degrees. The cloud structure looked loose enough to allow us escape routes once we got up into it. Harrisburg was still clamped down, but we prepared the airplane for a fast getaway and a flight to Norfolk.

The break came in mid-afternoon with a slight raising of the ceiling. Having warned the air traffic controllers that we would need an immediate return to Harrisburg should we discover no way through the ice, we took off and climbed aggressively into the weather. And we found a way through. Slipping and twisting to stay clear of the heaviest clouds, we passed Philadelphia and Wilmington. Near Baltimore, we began to see a bit of the ground—glimpsed through holes in the clouds, a patch of brown farmland, a forest of leafless trees, a stretch of sad gray water and marshland. Fifty miles later, over the middle of Chesapeake Bay, we ran entirely out of weather and changed our destination to Richmond, where we landed, refueled, and rethought the storm.

We went back into it after dark on a round trip to Wilkes-Barre, Pennsylvania, where the weather looked worst. The flight was not dangerous, but it was rough and involved. Again, ice was the problem. The stationary front had turned warm and was moving up the Eastern seaboard. In the blackness of the clouds we took ice and shed it, and kept repeating the cycle. At Wilkes-Barre we flew the instrument approach through cloud and falling snow, saw the runway lights, and pulled up without landing in order to avoid delays on the ground. Deep in the weather, we turned south for Richmond.

It was late at night. The storm had developed with unexpected strength. We stayed low, fighting forty-mile-per-hour head winds at 3,000 feet. To the left, the only other pilots on the frequency, a Delta crew, got blown off the instrument approach into Allentown and had to circle back to try again. Despite the south winds, the air temperature at our altitude was a frigid fifteen degrees. The clouds were thick with moisture. Outside of Philadelphia, with a splatter that sounded like sleet, we began to ice heavily. I shined a light on the wing and saw the ice growing like a voracious parasite. It looked white and crusty on the leading edge and clear where it streamed back over the wing. Within a minute we had taken more than an inch—a rate of accumulation that required immediate action. We gambled on a quick climb to 7,000, where we found warm Georgian air that melted the ice and slid it in sheets from the wings.

Had the gamble of that climb not paid off, and fast, we would have fallen back on our second plan—a quick retreat downwind into the frigid air to the north and a high-speed approach to a long runway. The high speed would have been necessary because iced-over wings stall at above-normal speeds. It would have complicated the landing, but we knew the airplane and thought if we could make the pavement, we could come to a safe stop.

All that proved to be academic, however. Having found the layer of warm air, we crept comfortably through the clouds to Richmond, welcoming the moisture rolling up our windshield, listening to the first reports of freezing rain on the surface in New Jersey. In the morning we saw the headlines about an unexpected ice storm in New York. People as usual were blaming forecasters for the mess.

PITY THE FORECASTERS. Of all the sciences, theirs is the most public. Here is a short version of its evolution. Emergence from the sea came first, followed by speech, followed by talk about the weather. Then came sacrificial rites, followed by the idea that peasants might pay a tithe to priests to keep the sky in order. Aristotle had the brains to separate the atmosphere from the heavens. He wrote *Meteorologica,* the first unified weather theory, around 340 BC. Two thousand years later, René Descartes doubted his methods and applied new rigor to the ignoring of God. In 1637, as an appendix to *Discours de la méthode,* he published "Les Météores," an explanation of the weather. Modern meteorology is essentially his child. Descartes suffered from a lack of weather data, since in the seventeenth century the basic instruments for measuring the air were still being invented. Credit Galileo with the thermometer, his student Torricelli with the barometer, and French intellectuals in general with the discovery that atmospheric pressure rises and falls with weather and altitude. Acknowledge various Europeans for their wind and humidity instruments, for their discoveries in physics, then jump to the mid-1800s, to places like Ohio, where the telegraph suddenly allowed news about the weather to travel faster than the weather itself.

National governments now set up weather services to collect observations and issue forecasts. At last a modern relationship could develop between the weather wizards and the public they served. It was a terrible shock. In England, the esteemed meteorologist and admiral Robert Fitzroy, who had captained Darwin's *Beagle* on the famous voyage of scientific discovery, was in 1855 named director of the first British weather office. Fitzroy was a good man, but like other nineteenth-century meteorologists he suffered from some misleading ideas about the nature of storm systems. Over the next ten years, he issued a series of dramatically bad forecasts. When the public finally noticed, a popular new sport was born. Fitzroy's last forecast was apparently the worst. Ridiculed by loftier scientists, attacked in the press, he did the right thing and shot himself. Maybe his old friend Darwin could have explained why forecasters today seem less sensitive.

Some seem almost belligerent. At the Camp Springs Operations Center, I asked the forecaster in the office next to Paul Kocin's about the kind of forecasts that gave him satisfaction. He fixed me with a hostile stare.

Satisfaction?

In the winter, he wanted to know about his damned drive home from the office. In the summer, he wanted to know about his damned backyard barbecue. That was enough for him. He did not expect the National Weather Service to organize his life for him. In the days leading up to his daughter's outdoor wedding the weather was unsettled, and so rather than complaining about the forecast he put up a damned tent.

He was a wounded man. As I left he said, "If people would just verify *all* our forecasts, all the times we call for *no* rain and get it right, they'd find our accuracy skills somewhere above 90 percent."

Naturally. Most weather is good, most of the time. This means that most forecasting is inherently easy. For instance, I predict that Las Vegas will be hot and sunny on July 4, 2026. And at small risk, I can go farther. My forecast for Nashville on the same day is: partly sunny, high near ninety-two degrees, chance of afternoon thundershowers. Also, I think I'll issue a flood watch.

I mentioned my confidence to Keith Seitter, the assistant director of the venerable American Meteorological

Society, based in Boston. He had a more philosophical attitude than the angry forecaster in Camp Springs. He said, "Sure, but we know those aren't the calls that buy us dinner. We get paid for the good storms, the ones where we say, 'Okay, the time has come to batten down the hatches.'"

Poor Fitzroy. He stumbled away from dinner in 1861, about fifty years early. At the start of the twentieth century a Norwegian mathematician named Vilhelm Bjerknes made an assertion that only then became obvious: The future form of the weather is determined entirely by its original form, acted on by the known mechanical and thermal laws of physics. This meant that numerical weather prediction was theoretically possible—you could start with a numerical map of a storm, and then apply a few equations.

Vilhem Bjerknes and his son Jacob began working through the initial problems of quantification. They came to the conclusion—and forced the meteorological establishment to come to it as well—that the existing models were completely unable to explain the observable life cycle of storms. In the 1920s they shook the establishment again by proving the importance of air-mass boundaries, which they called fronts, and by providing a conclusive mechanical explanation of the weather's behavior which recognized storms as atmospheric waves.

Simple but functional numerical models might now be built, but a practical problem remained in a world before computers. The volume of calculations was so large that the process of forecasting was slower than the weather itself. To predict even the simplest storm only a single day ahead could take months of calculations. One British theoretician imagined a "weather factory" in which 64,000 math workers, directed by the meteorological equivalent of a symphonic conductor, could barely keep up with the weather. And he vastly underestimated the problem. No wonder John von Neuman turned, in 1947, to weather forecasting as the perfect application for his new electronic computer. In April 1950, in Aberdeen, Maryland, under the guidance of von Neuman and meteorologist Jule Charney, the first successful numerical weather forecast was produced by a computer. Within a few years the computer results looked better than those of human forecasters.

That wasn't saying much. Theoretical understanding of the weather had advanced in recent decades, but under the pressure of a daily schedule, the forecasters still had to rely on gut feeling—the old-fashioned experience of having seen some weather pattern before. They called it the "analog approach" but might more honestly have called it educated guesswork. The results were poor for the obvious reason that no two storms are ever the same. A weather pattern today that looks like one last year will become something quite different by tomorrow.

Computers promised to solve those problems by bypassing the external features and working with the elemental equations of the weather process. The models were like electronic atmospheres within which mathematical storms could blossom. Meteorology suddenly knew no limits.

With refinement of the models and closer weather observation, forecasters would be able to look a week, a month—why not an entire year into the future? The public would adore them. Until recently, faith in these principles was so great that you could almost overlook a persistent problem with the product: In practice, the computer forecasts still had to be judged and touched up with the old and unreliable methods. The models kept getting better, providing measurable improvements in the accuracy of short-range forecasts. But beyond one or two days, major inaccuracies crept in; and beyond five days, the forecasts proved nearly worthless. They still do.

The natural response was to blame the models or the sparseness of data. But already by the 1960s, an MIT meteorologist named Edward Lorenz had taken a different approach. He wondered whether the computers had so perfectly captured the functioning of the atmosphere that the forecasting errors were a manifestation of some unknown trait of the weather itself. Lorenz reduced a computer model to its essentials, then ran weather simulations from seemingly identical starting points. The results on the computer, as in the real weather, were wildly diverging patterns.

It was a fascinating observation. No wonder the new forecasts kept going wrong. Individuality appeared to be as fundamental to computer-generated storms as to those of the actual sky. Lorenz kept reducing the problem until he entered the realm of theoretical mathematics. There, he isolated the hidden and fundamental trait that he called chaos. You could say that pilots knew it all along: The weather is wide beyond the continents and wild beyond prediction. But Lorenz went farther than that. By separating chaos from its atmospheric effects, by giving it clear mathematical expression, he made one of the most important discoveries of our time.

And forecasters are bitter about it. The scientific recognition of chaos has only added to their personal gloom. Whatever hope they harbored of public adoration has now faded. They take it particularly badly that Lorenz was not awarded the Nobel Prize. Physicists and philosophers may glory in uncertainty, but meteorologists are scorned even in Scandinavia because by Monday they cannot be sure of Sunday's weather. Chaos could let them off the hook, if anyone cared to let that happen, but of course no one does. The Weather Service's recent lengthening of the forecast from five days to seven was the last cruel reflex of an old dream. The fact is that no improvement in the model and no amount of computer power can fix such a forecast.

So, quietly, there has been a shift. Gone is the talk of clairvoyance. The effort turns inward now to improved radars and automated observation posts designed not to extend the length of the forecast but to narrow its geographic scale. It may be possible, say the visionaries, to anticipate individual thunderstorms a few hours in advance. Chaos theory still permits that. The wild talk now imagines personal forecasts that will follow people across their daily navigational grids.

How tedious.

But rise above your disdain and remember Fitzroy. And pity the forecasters who are paid to predict the weekend's weather. Lorenz has explained why they will get it wrong.

RICHMOND IN THE MORNING was cloudy. The Weather Service had an office at the airport, and so we walked in to sample the informed opinion there. One of us made a joke about the unexpected freezing rain in New York. The forecasters acted offended and refused to talk. We looked at their maps. The storm center had floated east from the Mississippi River to the hills of West Virginia. The warm front of the night before had buckled and jammed against New England's stubborn winter. Just below it, the mid-Atlantic states remained locked in ice and would be for the rest of the day. However, a classic cold front now curved south from the storm center along the western slope of the Appalachians and out across Jackson, Mississippi, and into the Gulf of Mexico. The front was moving slowly and packing weather: Reported ceilings were low, and radar showed lines of building rainstorms that were especially active near Knoxville, Tennessee. We decided to try the storm at its roughest.

After climbing from Richmond through warm cloud layers, we flew past Raleigh to the point over coastal North Carolina where we could turn west and head directly for the front. The route from there would take us over the heights of the Smoky Mountains, past Asheville, North Carolina, and down into Knoxville, where within the hour the airport had reported a 500-foot overcast and 2 miles visibility in heavy rain.

Westbound through the cloud tops at 8,000 feet, we crawled toward the mountains against sixty-mile-per-hour head winds. A dark wall marked the front ahead. As we approached, we made out bulbous and hooked cloud shapes indicating power and turbulence. Onboard the airplane we had a device, known as a stormscope, that plots the direction and distance to lightning strikes. It showed the first ones now, ahead about fifty miles. Lightning means thunderstorms. We strapped down hard into our seats.

The pilot's claim to have known always about chaos is of course a sort of vernacular conceit. Edward Lorenz discovered and could describe a core element in the very functioning of history. Pilots discover the immediate sky and can describe only their current confusion. That may explain the sensitivity of the Richmond forecasters, who, working at an airport office, must have been tired of listening to pilots' ignorance and presumption.

For example, this Carolina front into which we now prepared to fly was for meteorologists on the ground nothing dramatic or difficult to understand. A wedge of cold dry air was driving under warm moist air and forcing it up to altitudes where it cooled and condensed into cloud droplets, which collected into rain. Within the clouds, the condensation released the moist air's store of latent heat in a molecular process opposite to that of evaporative cooling. The released heat caused the air to rise higher and condense faster, which in turn released more heat. Accelerated in places by uplift from the mountains, the chain reaction raged along the entire length of the front.

When later Paul Kocin studied my weather map, he said, "Yup, a cold front." He glanced at me with the disappointment I had come to expect. "But you know, it really wasn't anything unusual."

He was right. It was like flying into a slow, sustained explosion. The rain pounded at the windshield and tore paint from the wing's leading edges. Turbulence slammed the airplane from above and below, rocked it onto its side, stretched us against the seatbelts, and at times shook the instrument panel so violently that we had trouble focusing on the instruments. But that makes it sound worse than it was. You can fly an airplane like you ride a horse, refusing to be intimidated. It is one of the inside tricks of storm flying—based on the knowledge that airplanes are the most weather-worthy of vehicles, strong and capable beyond the imagination even of their pilots.

Passengers are not easily reassured because in the alien world of flight they lack a useful sense of scale. But here is some advice for nervous airline riders: The only reason to grip your seat is to keep the seatbelt from bruising your thighs. It may help in reverse to know that the trickiest turbulence is not rough at all but is the layered shift in the wind known by pilots as shear, which happens close to the ground and causes a notoriously seamless sink. There are solutions for that, too.

It was just as well that we had no passengers for Knoxville. Our ride kept getting rougher. The pilots with me were apparently unafraid. The man at the controls fist-fought the airplane with determination. I watched him carefully, alert for fatigue or any slackening of control. We measured the head winds in places now at eighty miles an hour. The clouds were swollen with rain and so dark that we switched on the cockpit lights. The weather at Asheville, one of our escapes if the weather became unflyable, had dropped nearly to the limits of the instrument approach.

We considered diverting while we still could but got a report that Knoxville, ahead, was holding steady. We continued westward. As we crossed the highest mountains, the stormscope showed lightning strikes off the right wing and ahead to the left. We heard the crackling on the radio. Lightning is an electrical reckoning. When it occurs between oppositely charged clouds, or between the clouds and the ground, airplanes will not get in the way. But airplanes do get hit by lightning—or a mild form of the same thing. As they fly through heavy rain or snow, they build up a static charge which normally bleeds off through metal wicks attached to the trailing edges. But if the wicks can't keep up, the charge builds until, with a flash and a bang, a stroke of lightning takes care of it. The stroke will usually not ignite the fuel, but it may damage a circuit or—as occurred to me during that first winter of my cargo flying—burn or blow small holes in the airplane. Airplane repairs are expensive. So we grew concerned when, with lightning around, the rain turned to sleet and our radios started hissing with static and began to fade. It was a sign that the wicks could no longer keep up.

The static charge grew so large that eventually it

knocked out our ability to talk to air traffic control. This was less of a problem than it might seem, since there were no other airplanes out there and the controllers could see us on radar and knew our intentions. The static charge continued to build. We grew more concerned when next we lost the navigational radios as well, one by one, until for a while we banged through the crashing rain and sleet by compass and clock alone.

It would be ridiculous to say that we were not then afraid. The sky had gathered around us in a malicious display of its power. But the control of fear is a necessary part of the inner work of flight, and one of the reasons no doubt that each of us was there. We still had an escape route open to us—a 180-degree turn and a retreat down-wind and down-weather, on compass alone if need be, into the warm coastal air of the Carolinas. We talked it over. We decided to keep going.

I tuned one radio to an inactive frequency and rhythmically keyed the transmitter, hoping to spark a discharge to help the static wicks dissipate the airplane's electrical shield. I don't know whether the trick worked, but we avoided any damaging strikes. Past the mountains the weather eased, the static wicks did their job, and the navigational radios sprang back crisply. Soon afterward we made contact with a Knoxville controller, who mentioned laconically that we seemed to have come through "some pretty good cells."

We had not seen the ground now for several hours. Angling for the approach into Knoxville, we descended rapidly through continuing rain and cloud. Ten miles north of the airport we hooked onto the instrument approach and began to ride its electronic beams like a downsloping rail to the runway. Five hundred feet off the ground, the clouds hinted at the green fields. Seconds later we caught the motion of trees sliding by below. The runway's pulsing approach lights materialized ahead, floating in the mist. We emerged from the clouds, crossed the runway threshold, and touched down on the glistening runway.

That afternoon we continued down the front in rain and ice, and spent the night in Montgomery, Alabama. By morning, the storm center had crossed Nantucket and was heading into the North Atlantic, where within a day, deprived of its sustaining temperature differences, it would quietly collapse into the Icelandic Low, the birthplace of European weather. The end of its weakened cold front curved through central Florida. We flew to Orlando and made an approach through gentle clouds that now seemed like old friends. Then we headed west and along the Gulf Coast finally flew into the clear skies behind the system. In mid-flight we radioed for a weather briefing. Already a powerful new system was bringing blizzards to the Great Lakes. The news encouraged us not to regret the old storm's passing. We turned north, in search again of our landscapes of solitude.

SIX

Slam and Jam

THOSE LANDSCAPES are internal, made up within the cockpit of a technical intimacy with the instruments, of concentration and self-control, of sheer distance from the ground. But there is another, entirely different landscape, an external and public one, which has resulted from our startling evolutionary success. Flight's greatest gift is to let us look around, and when we do we find that the sky has become crowded with others of our egocentric species, and that each of us wants to go first.

Nowhere is this more true than in the New York area, where the runways of Newark's International Airport, for instance, now rank among the most heavily used in the world. Night after day, in good weather and in bad, the airplanes bear down on them. Their traffic is relentless. Drivers on the adjacent New Jersey Turnpike can count on the distraction: the procession of lights inbound to the runway, the graceful touchdowns, the taxiway parades, the miraculous, banked, nose-high departures. The equipment out there is complex, capable, even exotic, but it is the sheer quantity of it that commands our attention. The big orange radar that stands beside the turnpike can never stop turning.

The radar sweeps the sky beyond the eye, keeping watch on the intertwined arrivals and departures from New York's three major airports. LaGuardia and Kennedy each handle a third of a million flights annually, and Newark, which used to be called Sleepy Hollow and is still thought of as a lesser airport, is in reality even busier than the others, accounting for another half-million flights a year. Because jets fly fast and turn wide, these three airports, which once stood distinctly apart, now lie atop one another. Adding to the tangle, each of the smaller airports— White Plains, Teterboro, and Islip, to name just three— produces its own heavy flows of arrivals and departures. And just overhead pass the en route flights cruising to and from Boston, Philadelphia, and Washington, D.C. The result is the most congested air space in the world, a chunk of sky through which much of American air traffic daily flies, a special place where the usually reliable "big sky" theory of collision avoidance simply does not apply.

It was because of the congestion that I chose Newark to flesh out my impression that, despite what the public has been led to believe, no immediate danger lurks within the system of air traffic control. This may come as a surprise. If there is one thing that nearly everyone can agree on, it is that air traffic control is critical to the safety of flight. Decades of moviemaking and superficial reporting have contributed to the idea that controllers "guide" airplanes, that the task allows no room for error or inattention, that controllers must have superhuman reflexes and cool nerves, that only split-second timing and fast computers keep disaster at bay, that passengers' lives hang in the balance because of old and unreliable equipment—and that the work of air traffic controllers as a consequence is impossibly burdensome. These images jibe so neatly with people's sense of helplessness in flight that they have acquired the force of an accepted reality and have become the necessary starting point for any conversation about air traffic control.

But that reality is a myth. Controllers do not puncture it because it gives them leverage with the public and because they themselves have come to believe in it. To be sure, the potential for collisions exists, all the more so in the high-pressure environment of the big-city sky. Concern for safety is the bottom line of all aviation—in the control room as well as in the cockpit. But even in a place like New York, the controllers' real concern is with a set of work rules which operate narrowly atop the nearly absolute safety provided already by pilots and aircraft designers. Mistakes by controllers have led to accidents, but only as one link in a chain of failures. Air traffic control's main function is to provide for the efficient flow of traffic and to allow for the best possible use of limited runway space—in other words, not to keep people alive but to keep them moving.

Like jugglers, controllers are practiced at handling constellations of flying objects. There is an important difference, though. When jugglers get distracted, their constellations tumble to the ground, but when controllers make mistakes, or lose their radars or radios, their airplanes continue to fly. Even if these jugglers were to stop suddenly and walk away, the elements of their constellations would on their own eventually slow down, take in the situation more or less calmly, and by following a variety of well-accepted procedures discover places where they could land softly. Imagine juggling on a low-gravity planet using smart balls that knew how to navigate and to talk to one another and could find ways not to collide.

Of course, once the balls landed they would not rise again without the juggler. That, too, is the nature of air traffic control. Controllers have to work well and willingly in order to keep the growing air transportation system aloft. And only the most persistent glad-talker would deny that over the past decades controllers have had difficulty, for whatever reason, in living up to the demands placed upon them. But air traffic control's core problems are both less tangible and more difficult to resolve. Yes, the hardware can be modernized, and with sufficient political support new airports can be built, but air traffic control's greatest weakness is cultural and organizational and will not yield to the microchip and the dollar. This weakness lies deep inside the Federal Aviation Administration, a government agency now divided into two mutually antagonistic camps, management and the working controllers, each with its own traditions and memories.

The FAA has other problems as well. It has been accused of waste and stupidity and on a regular basis has been held responsible for airline crashes because of its role in certifying airline and airport operations. In response, it has promised to streamline itself and to pay closer attention to detail; Congress has occasionally decreed other changes. But such reforms, to the extent that they touch it at all, only brush the surface of air traffic control, an individualistic profession which relies on the willingness and creativity of each on-duty controller but within which old-fashioned class resentments and labor discontent now rise like specters from the past. A generation has passed since the great controller strike of 1981, when Ronald Reagan fired most of the work force, giving the FAA the opportunity for a fresh start. But there is a new union now, the National Air Traffic Controllers Association (NATCA), and it is growing as angry as the old one. Among the controllers a quiet and as yet unseen rebellion has broken out. The consequences are serious, if not for safety then for something more important still—the routine human flight that already, after only a century, we have come to believe is our right.

ON A FIRST VISIT to the cavernous radar room of New York Approach, the noise, commotion, and apparent chaos seem to validate the worst fears about air traffic control. Certainly air traffic control has become more dynamic than it was in days gone by—the days of men with crew cuts and white shirts holding binoculars and saying "roger." Controllers today wear T-shirts and jeans and have adopted the swagger of the street. Most do not work in towers. This place called New York Approach, which has responsibility for the low altitudes above the entire metropolitan area, is situated away from the airports, half an hour past Kennedy on Long Island. It is known throughout the world for the fury of its controllers, especially those assigned to the Newark sector, who work in a condition of permanent frenzy—shouting, complaining, joking, throwing plastic data strips the length of the consoles, staring at their screens with gum-chewing concentration, swearing at their supervisors, punching the keyboards, gesturing at the radio transmissions of the pilots who cannot match their pace.

This is the sort of intense activity cited in cases of "burnout," and it obscures the actual functioning of air traffic control. I spent days at the Newark sector, absorbing the technical details, and came away with the appreciation that the intensity was mostly self-induced and was actually what many of the controllers thrived on. The opportunity to indulge in it seemed, in fact, to be what had drawn them to the job.

The controllers did complain about the pressures, but largely because they would have been embarrassed not to. They complained also about the food in the cafeteria, the condition of the roads, and life on Long Island. One man finally admitted, "How can you go home from this and be satisfied mowing the lawn?" It was practically a declaration of love. About the only time the controllers seemed genuinely upset was when they talked about their superiors in the FAA.

I don't mean to diminish the controllers or to belittle the experience and dedication they bring to the job. The sight of a radar scope swarming with little ovals, each representing a flight, is indeed daunting. But what does it mean that control rooms can sound like trading floors? Maybe only that air traffic control has become less regimented, more human, and more complex than originally anticipated. There is no doubt that air traffic control consists now of an accumulation of informal solutions pieced together at the last moment to cope with an overwhelming flow. In that sense it is a typically American institution—the problem coming first, the attempt to manage it coming afterward. And who knows, this may be for the best.

On a mechanical level, the most pressing issue that controllers face is a surge in air traffic without a commensurate expansion of runway availability. Since 1979, when President Jimmy Carter deregulated the airlines, unleashing competition among them, the number of scheduled flights in the United States has grown by nearly 70 percent. And the growth has been lopsided: Of the several thousand airplanes aloft during a typical daytime rush, most are headed for the same few cities. The busiest fifty airports, out of thousands of airports altogether, now account for more than 80 percent of the nation's traffic. The lopsidedness is in part a reflection of people's final destinations, but it also results from the airlines' competitive needs for efficient route structures centered on hubs—the now familiar passenger- and cargo-exchange airports that require flights to arrive and depart at about the same time, and that by their nature inflate the number of takeoffs and landings.

Newark, for instance, does double duty as a New York destination and as a Northeastern hub for Continental, United Parcel, and Federal Express. Faced with all the inbound airplanes, its controllers have no choice but to greet them. They grapple with the core problems of over-crowded air space—that flight is fast, fluid and deter-minedly forward-moving; that every airport, airplane, and pilot is different; that thunderstorms, fogs, winds, ice, snow, or merely low clouds can block a route or slow a runway; that even under a clear blue sky airline schedules push airports past their limits. The slightest bump then rip-ples backward, forcing the controllers to scramble. A flight may miss an early turnoff from a runway, or come in too fast or slow, or ignore a call on the radio, or jump out of line with an engine shut down. A new pilot may be unsure of the local procedures. An old pilot may get huffy and insist on having his way. These things happen constantly. The resulting complications are measured in wasted fuel, money, and time—but not in lives lost, or even in levels of danger.

Across the Newark controllers' radar screens I watched

the targets move in short jumps, dragging identifying tags behind them: Lufthansa, United, Continental—dozens of airplanes at a time. By assigning headings and descent paths, the controllers angled the flights down from the mid-altitude collection points known as arrival gates, joined them up to the south, and swept them into an arc which took them north past the airport and skirted LaGuardia's air space before bending back around, straight in for the runways. The purpose of the arc was only secondarily to keep the airplanes apart. Its primary purpose was nearly the opposite: to give controllers the angular flexibility necessary to tighten the spacing and to exploit the occasional gaps by shooting airplanes in from the side, pushing them toward the airport ahead of sequence.

The most basic geometry of air traffic dictates that departing airplanes naturally fan out and so usually diverge, that cruising airplanes only sometimes cross, but that arriving airplanes must inevitably converge. Moreover, the inbound traffic compresses accordion-style as the airplanes slow toward their touchdown speeds. The compression does not mean that the airplanes are in danger of rear-ending each other; closing speeds are low between airplanes flying in the same direction. The formal separation requirements, which are measured in miles, are dictated ultimately by the civilian orthodoxy that requires one airplane to taxi clear of the runway before the following airplane lands. Military pilots routinely take off and land in formation, and safely. I don't mean that airline pilots should, too, but that the margins built into standard civilian procedures are large. That is why, between themselves, New York Approach controllers take their pride not in the collisions they avoid—an issue that almost never comes up in the manner the public imagines—but in the pressure they keep on the runways.

AT THE RECEIVING END of that pressure stand the tower controllers at Newark International Airport. On the day I went to see them an overcast paved the sky. I wandered through the airport labyrinth to the service road that led between blast fences out across the vast concrete aprons toward the main runways. It was a bleak landscape, an industrial plain roamed by heavy machinery and scented by jet exhaust, a technical world that was practical and unadorned, a place to feel at home. At the end of the service road the control tower rose against oily winds.

The door at the base had a buzzer and was unattended. An elevator carried me up to the mid-level, where I met the tower's chief, an immaculate man who wore cuff links and a well-tailored suit in the typically dandified style of the FAA management. We sat in his government-issue office, with the clean desk and coffee table, the soft chairs, the FAA seal, the flag, the picture of the president. Drapes hid the view of the wasteland outside but could not exclude the roar of the jets, which regularly shook the walls. Airplanes were backed up fifteen-deep on the taxiways and for 200 miles out into the arrival flow. The chief volunteered that Newark had in recent times led the nation in delays, but he said the airport had improved its record for the current fiscal year. I asked him to be specific about the changes he had made. He admitted that the improvement was due mostly to an unusual stretch of good weather. I assured him that as a pilot I understood. I wanted him not to make the kind of excuses that would embarrass us both. You can do only so much with three cramped runways, and you can do less when the weather turns bad. Controllers do not fly airplanes. Controllers do not control the climate.

I rode the elevator higher and climbed the steel stairs into the tower's cab, the small glass-walled room where the work is done. The cab held a dozen controllers, ordinary-looking men in casual clothes, the sort of standard middle Americans bred by the outer city. In a shopping mall crowd you would never have picked them out. But if they were ordinary men, they were in this place, on the job, also impressively unsettled. Disdaining the swivel chairs, they worked on their feet, tethered by their headset cords, moving restlessly along the radio consoles, leaning toward the traffic outside, checking the radar scopes, issuing instructions, asking questions, barking into telephones, joking, swearing, shouting across the cab in a confusion of emotions difficult for any outsider to decipher.

At the center of the turmoil stood a slight young man with blond hair and birdlike reactions whom I will call Dobkin. He wore a lightweight headset and held a transmitter switch down low in his right hand. It was Dobkin's turn on the frequency known as "local," which gave him responsibility for the airport's two parallel runways, the narrowly spaced "22 Left" and "22 Right," running southwest beside the turnpike. The third runway, a short east-west reliever called "29," crossed the thresholds of the parallels and conflicted with their traffic. It was a cramped and awkward layout.

Dobkin said, "We work with what we've got. The parallels were built way too close for simultaneous approaches. We use the outer runway for arrivals. We use the inner runway for departures. We try to run the props over there on 29, keep them out of the way of the jets, but we can't cross them into the main approach. When the wind's light we flip that runway back and forth, pump a load of departures to the west, then bring the inbounds around for landings to the east."

The idea that such a controller is somehow in the business of "talking airplanes down" is the part of the myth fostered by the movies. Dobkin had ridden in cockpits a few times, but he knew little about the actual flying of airplanes. Between transmissions he told me how he had come to the job after a stint as a controller in the Navy. He had escaped home, had learned a skill, had grown tired of saluting, and had hired on with the FAA because the FAA was hiring. He had chosen a control tower over a radar room because he liked to look at airplanes. He had picked Newark for the money and action, and he sometimes now wished that he hadn't. He concluded his story with the false regret of a man proud of his skills: "So here I am ten years later, just another keeper of the concrete."

He had a high-strung personality, encouraged by the work. If the purpose of his game was simple—to squeeze the maximum possible use from these three runways—in execution it was fast-paced, complex, and competitive. He said, "The hard part's not doing it, but doing it right. You've got to use every chance, every gap, to move the traffic. Slam and jam. The job keeps you on your toes."

And safety? It intruded not as an active minute-by-minute concern but as a set of rules within which he had to perform, the most basic of which was the restriction against simultaneous operations on a single runway. Perspective is needed here. The deadliest airline accident in history was a runway accident that occurred in 1977, when two 747s collided on Tenerife (in a fog, one taking off, the other taxiing across); and other runway collisions have occurred. They have all, however, been freakish accidents resulting from multiple errors by both the controllers and the pilots. Except in the worst weather, or sometimes at night, pilots can easily see anyone lingering on the runway and on their own initiative can delay their takeoffs, or if they are landing can add power and climb safely away from the ground. It is primarily because such go-arounds waste valuable landing slots and further burden the final approach that controllers work to avoid them. In other words, Dobkin took the timing seriously, but as an efficient practitioner of traffic flow rather than out of a sense of averting disaster.

I had been told at the FAA headquarters in Washington that the capacity of Newark's runways was 180 operations

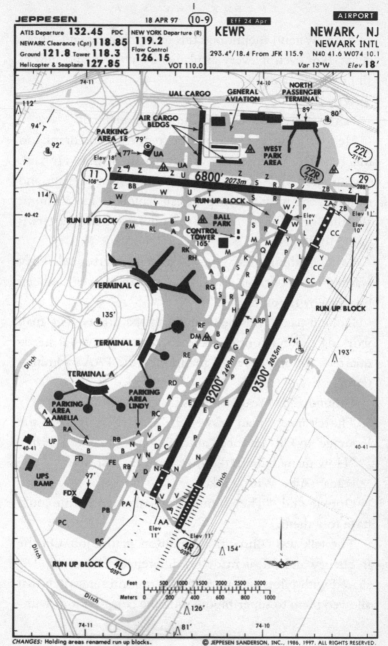

JEPPESEN   18 APR 97   (10-9)   Eff 24 Apr   **KEWR**   **NEWARK, NJ**
AIRPORT
NEWARK INTL

ATIS Departure **132.45** PDC	NEW YORK Departure (R) **119.2**
NEWARK Clearance (Cpt) **118.85**	Flow Control
Ground **121.8** Tower **118.3**	**126.15**
Helicopter & Seaplane **127.85**	VOT **110.0**

293.4°/18.4 From JFK 115.9   N40 41.6 W074 10.1

Var 13°W   Elev **18'**

an hour. When I mentioned this to Dobkin he said, "For-get it. Not even if every airplane's a 737-400, and they're all flown the same."

Why the 400?"

"Land short, slow fast, hit the high-speed exit."

He took a short break from the frequency and drank too much coffee. Washington's arrogance ate at him. He said, "A hundred and eighty? With all three runways up and running, the most this airport can handle is 120 an hour. Weather slows us to 70. You tell me how headquarters is going to do better."

I said, "I think they've got ideas about personnel. They warned me about this place. They said the tower has been hijacked by union hotheads."

Dobkin passed this news along to the others. The man working ground control asked about my sources at head-quarters. Among others, I mentioned the FAA's adminis-trator.

Ground said, "Yeah? Who is he this week?"

The clearance man answered, "He's the guy with the 'courage' to kill 'advanced automation.' Didn't you hear?"

"How many billions did they burn on that one?"

Radar said, "What a joke."

Dobkin said, "They should have asked you. You could have told them."

The talk was constant, a condition of the job. On the frequency and off, it made no difference. The controllers shared with pilots an ease with the transmitter switch that allowed them to superimpose multiple conversations without mixing the lines. At the back of the tower cab, the shift supervisor listened quietly with the placidity of a commander who could no longer keep the pace. A trainee came around with a takeout menu from a cheap Chinese restaurant. Dobkin was cruel to him. In his presence he said, "Here's a guy who just can't get the picture, but because this is the FAA he'll never wash out. It's a program they call 'Train to Succeed.'"

I did not mention what Dobkin seemed to have forgotten—that "Train to Succeed" had been a union initiative.

The airport beyond the glass walls crawled with airplanes moving slowly toward the runways. Thousands of passengers sat like patient prisoners strapped into their seats, but Dobkin's attention went first to the traffic pouring down the final approach. He judged the inbound lights with a familiar mixture of confidence and concentration.

The inbounds tonight showed up first on the tower's radar screen, where we watched the work of an unseen Approach controller who was pushing the flights closer together than the runways would be able to handle for any length of time. Dobkin asked the pilots for speed reductions, which worked at first but soon echoed backward. The tower supervisor telephoned Approach for better service and was told irritably that Approach itself was being force-fed by the long-distance controllers over at New York Center, who in turn were squabbling with their counterparts in Cleveland. In the meantime, because of Teterboro and LaGuardia traffic, New York Approach could not swing the Newark inbounds any wider. Approach threatened to make space by freezing the "commuter" turboprop departures off of Runway 29, a restriction which would have crowded the turboprop departures over to the parallels.

There simply was not enough space for all the airplanes, not in the air and not on the ground—at least not without delays. Dobkin cursed Approach nonetheless. He thought he was doing the controllers there a favor by cleaning up their mess on final. So far he had avoided any wasteful go-arounds, but the airplanes now were barely clearing the runway before the traffic behind flared down across the threshold. After a Delta flight checked in with a stately drawl, Dobkin knocked twenty knots off the Continental that followed. To me he said, "You learn to read the signs." Delta dawdled after landing. Off the radio Dobkin snapped, "Come on dumb boy, clear the runway." Delta did and Continental landed short, with company behind.

The unfortunate consequence of Dobkin's success was the speed with which it was filling up the airport. To make room for the new arrivals, ground control kept pushing loaded airplanes up the taxiways toward the departure runway, 22 Right. Dobkin cleared them for takeoff as aggressively as spacing within the outbound corridor allowed. With relief provided by Runway 29, the tower had managed to avoid gridlock on the ground; nonetheless, the departure delays were steadily growing longer. The reason had to do with aircraft performance: While descent angles and final approach speeds can be matched for most inbound traffic, optimal climb rates and speeds vary widely between departing airplanes; moreover, because the heaviest airplanes generate dangerous wakes immediately after liftoff, additional spacing behind them is required.

For Dobkin the result was an inevitable irregularity in takeoff timing which translated into the inefficient use of 22 Right. Ground control worked to reduce the effect by bunching airplanes by type so that they could be launched in quick order. The success of this strategy then created another problem: Having landed on 22 Left and pulled onto the taxiways between the runways, the arrivals could not cross the departure runway to get to the terminals. They accumulated between the runways until, by threatening to block the runway exits for landing traffic, they forced Dobkin to hold the takeoffs. Dobkin tried hard to avoid such hangups by exploiting the natural gaps in the departure flow. He said, "It's Traffic 101. You cross behind a heavy jet, a seven-two, a prop. You use every chance you've got. You don't forget any part of it. You *keep* this traffic moving."

What he did *not* say was, "You keep this traffic apart."

Not that the lives-hanging-by-a-thread idea was entirely absent. I asked Dobkin about the toll on controllers in shattered health, divorce, and drink. "Sure," he said uncomfortably. "It's hard sometimes—I've known guys who had to get out."

Earlier a controller had said to me, "Stressed out? If you're the type, sure. But then it's the freeway traffic when you're driving to work that will really do it to you."

* * *

PILOTS DO NOT BELIEVE that air traffic control is in the business of keeping them alive, or that it should be. This is not a matter of principle or bravado but simple observation. The surrounding sky is so large that even when another airplane passes nearby it remains by comparison very small. Like other pilots who fly in crowded air space, I have had close calls with traffic. But "close" can mean many things. Is it a crossing that surprises you, or one that requires an evasive maneuver, or one so tight and fast that no maneuver is possible? Or is it—most likely—merely the violation of an official standard that may to some extent be arbitrary? I talked to a controller involved in research with radar simulations, who said, "You'd be amazed how hard it is to vector two airplanes into each other." The sort of head-on encounter in which another airplane appears as a dot and within ten or twenty seconds fills your windshield is very rare. Neither pilots nor controllers need gunslinger reflexes. Airplanes sidle slowly toward each other. Can you wonder why a pilot would feel detached from the newspaper and television treatments of his experience? Airplanes will continue to collide, but the reporters who speak so urgently of confusion aloft, of all the accidents avoided by chance, seem to have discovered some separate sky.

Moment-by-moment air traffic control has less to do with the safe operation of the airplane than with the forward progress of flight. From tower control, to radar, to tower again, a procession of voices accompanies each airplane across the map. Their presence is humanized by accents, moods, and informalities and by a shared sense of accommodation and competence. Good controllers are neither automatons nor traffic cops. At the start of a trip they deliver a "clearance," assigning the pilots a computer-generated route to the destination. In an uncrowded sky such a clearance might stand alone as a guarantee of traffic-free flying, eliminating the need for controllers. In the actual sky, it serves instead as a plan in the event of radio failure and as an approximate prediction for the actual flight path.

The details fill in after takeoff. Controllers thread the departing airplanes through the first busy altitudes with headings and climb restrictions. Pilots are expected not to comply blindly but rather to judge and agree. They distinguish between the controllers' wrongs and rights. By visualizing the subtleties of a changing technical geography, they can even predict their instructions.

Eventually the pilots are turned loose to proceed high and fast on course, either along the airways that zigzag across the grid of navigational stations on the ground or, more commonly, in airplanes equipped with independent long-range navigational devices, directly toward the destination. Over the continental United States, the airplanes cruise under the surveillance of "centers"—en route radar facilities whose role, despite the increase in traffic, remains less interventionist than passengers might imagine. Across a sky so deep and wide, "control" consists mostly of monitoring flights as they proceed by routes and altitudes that have been approved by the computers but that remain essentially the pilot's or airline's choice. With controllers' routine approval, pilots cut corners, deviate around thunderstorms, ride good winds, slide above or below the reports of turbulence. Controllers intervene if they see a traffic conflict developing, or if other controllers elsewhere ask for delays or route changes. The respective roles are clearly defined: Controllers may separate airplanes, but pilots still navigate them.

Controllers do make errors, routinely. Pilots judge the errors, just as in turn the controllers judge theirs. For the participants it is hardly worth commenting on. Few of the errors are serious. The system works in any case only because of the unspoken compensation that goes on within it, the subjective reading of the traffic and the endless adjustments that define the art for everyone involved. You play with speed and descent rates, with bank angles and headings; you measure your transmissions and words; you anticipate the other pilots, their skills and their airplanes; you calibrate the controllers in their own calibrations of you. Busy air space functions on the inside like an ethereal community, a radio village rich with understandings. Machines move through it, but it is a community of the mind.

It is obvious that you cannot just elbow your way through bad weather and into crowded airports. Still, let us imagine a total collapse, one day, of the nation's entire air traffic control system. Even then, airplanes would not simply begin to blunder helplessly into each other. Transportation would of course grind to a halt and the nation would soon be paralyzed, but safety would probably not be affected. Pilots in flight would sit up and pay attention, but they would continue to fly and navigate normally. They would find frequencies on the maps, and talk to their airline dispatchers, and radio to each other as they do already at the many uncontrolled airports. If they were originally headed for hubs like Newark or O'Hare, they might turn and fly somewhere else. Some would have to revert to cumbersome arrival routes, and many would have to hold for a while. But few pilots would feel seriously threatened. This is all the more true in modern cockpits equipped with traffic displays. In the airplane I fly today, I often spot other airplanes electronically (not to mention by looking outside) before the controllers call them out to me.

Certainly the air traffic control system has become an ill-planned patchwork with geographic overlaps, conflicting procedures, and chance redundancies that exist as remnants of earlier times. Airplanes move from one little zone of control to the next, are spoken to across overloaded voice-radio frequencies, are handed off from one controller to another, and are given the sort of customized service that often preempts the needs of the larger traffic flow. Individual control facilities function as parallel fiefdoms, each with its own traditions, procedures, and compromises, each speaking directly to (and quarreling with) its neighbors, without passing through a central command. If you were to design a system from scratch, you would never design this. Nonetheless, one consequence of the system's haphazard structure, of its decentralization and its very inefficiency, is to scatter its many failures, and to provide pilots and controllers with a rich weave of choices when something goes wrong—a radio quits, a radar quits, a computer stops calculating. Perhaps partly as a result, no air traffic control equipment failure has ever yet caused an accident.

I do not mean that the hardware is good enough but that as an educated user I do not feel threatened by its imperfections. Within such a large and complex system, we can assume that the equipment will wear out or become obsolete and that the government will compound the problem by reacting incompetently. It is of course absurd that the FAA has not yet replaced all the old unreliable IBM computers that contain routing information for flights. And it is annoying that the addition of new power supplies in several centers caused outages that in turn led to major delays. And it is disgraceful that the FAA wasted hundreds of millions of dollars between an overambitious attempt to consolidate control rooms and a poorly managed, ill-conceived, and now abandoned "advanced automation system"—an attempt to automate a wide range of internal air traffic control transactions. But on what basis, exactly, do people care that a controller's radar display does not contain the processing power of a personal computer? And why, precisely, do we worry that backup flight information is still written out on strips of paper? And what was the point, technically, when a secretary of transportation, who was an ex-mayor of Denver, held up an old vacuum tube for ridicule? The controllers, whose workplace he meant to improve, are said to have jeered at his theatrics.

Even he must have known that vacuum tubes are not the problem.

THE REAL PROBLEM lies not in hardware but in human relations. From its origins in the 1920s among the agencies responsible for the fresh and bewildering endeavor of human flight, the FAA developed an institutional personality, unrestrained by history or tradition, that was raw, arrogant, and domineering—an exuberant expression, some observers still believe, of the twentieth-century form of big government. For generations most controllers came from the military, bringing with them a hierarchical view of organization, which was further encouraged by the nature of the work. The managers were controllers who worked their way up through the ranks, taking pride in each small step, savoring the distinctions which marked their rise. Those distinctions may have been subtle at first, but they grew and strengthened and eventually came to define the management's style.

To explain the resulting tensions then and now, a controller in New York mimicked his bosses for me. He said, "When I was a controller, I worked aircraft. It was easy. I told them what to do and they did it. Now that I'm management, I work controllers. Same deal. I tell *you* what to do and *you* do it."

But by the 1970s, a younger generation of controllers was no longer willing to comply. Faced with a rebellious work force, the bewildered FAA management commissioned a psychiatrist, Robert Rose, then of Boston University, to conduct a study of controllers' mental health. The Rose report, published in 1978, confirmed the popular impression that controllers had stressful jobs (they suffered disproportionately from hypertension and certain psychological difficulties, including uncontrollable anger and anti-social behavior), but it concluded in typically stilted language that the causes had less to do with the pressures of traffic than with divisiveness within the FAA: "This finding of 'It's not so much what they are doing as the context in which they are doing it' holds definite implications for changes that might be considered in the work environment to reduce the risk for future morbidity."

In short, the problem lay with the way the FAA was run. Then came deregulation and the steady growth of air traffic. At New York Approach, a controller with tattooed forearms and a ponytail told me his insider's history of the Newark sector. He meant it as the insider's history of all air traffic control. He said, "For years you're sitting around Sleepy Hollow eating your brown bag lunches, then one day you look up and, Jesus, you've got a hundred airplanes inbound and every one of them is low on fuel."

This happened with the deregulation of the airlines, when People Express, then Continental and others, rushed into the Newark void. The controller said, "The managers and headquarters types, the paper-pushers, they would have run away. The only reason the system survived was the skill of the guys working the mikes. They dropped their sandwiches. They threw away their manuals. They stood up to the traffic. They managed to patch things together."

The real history is less tidy, because nationwide in 1981 most of those same valiant controllers went on strike and lost their jobs, and it was then the turn of the managers and headquarters types, emerging from the back offices and reviving old skills, to stand up to the traffic for the year that followed. The pressure was eased by a stopgap reservation system and an enforced reduction in flights. Nonetheless, to everyone's surprise, the managers actually did as good a job of controlling as had all those "irreplaceable" union members. Working with small and enthusiastic teams, they handled nearly as many airplanes, safely, and demonstrated convincingly that parts of the old system had indeed been overstaffed. But to accomplish this they, too, had to "throw away the manuals." For several years after the strike very little of the normal paperwork got done.

It should have been a lesson but was not. The frustrating part of this story is that after the FAA hired and trained a new and smaller work force of "permanent replacements," the managers returned to their offices and again lost respect for the job.

The permanent replacements—strikebreakers by another name—were naturally compliant at first. They were blank slates, the sort of fresh young recruits harboring hopes for promotion who could have been made to share the perspectives of friendly, flexible, and competent management. They gave the FAA an opportunity that other troubled organizations can only dream of—to shed the burdens of the past and move beyond outdated concepts of hierarchy and conflict. But quickly then the recruits became working controllers and came face to face with the airline boom, the congestion around hub airports, the front-line problems of sequencing converging airplanes. To keep the traffic moving, they had to disregard a growing stream of impractical directives from the managers. There was no mystery to why the pre-strike pattern of distance, distrust, and hostility was reasserting itself (everyone involved knew the history), but it seemed all the worse for its institutional inevitability. At New York Approach, I met two brothers—one a manager, the other a controller—who had stopped speaking to each other because of it. In their anger and intractability I could see the emotionalism dividing all air traffic control.

The resentment today is so strong that for many controllers their hatred of the FAA has become a burden against which the original pleasures of the job—the "slam and jam" and giving of good service—has to be weighed. A controller from California wrote this to me:

> You seemed to be surprised that controllers now have a vested interest in the failure or embarrassment of the FAA. But "they" have taken our profession and our air traffic control and completely screwed it up. "They" have blown every opportunity to do what is right. "They" have devoted their efforts to the goddess Bureaucracy. "They" have relegated us to second class status. "They" have completely forgotten why "they" and "we" are here.

Management, for its part, must cope with a profound political uncertainty. This is usually explained as a confusion between two missions—the need simultaneously to promote and to regulate civil aviation—and though Congress has eliminated the agency's formal responsibility for promotion, that confusion remains real. But the political uncertainty also stems in many cases from something even more difficult to legislate away: the managers' envy of their natural adversaries, the unfettered executives of the airline industry. Those executives are the same people who crowd airline passengers into hub airports and then denounce the FAA for the resulting delays. And the FAA does not really disagree.

The politics play like a cultural revolution in which disdain for government becomes an orthodoxy required of the government itself. This, too, we can now see in the still, fresh realm of the sky. Moreover, it is generally agreed that airline deregulation is an experiment that has worked and that the very growth of traffic is one proof of it. When forced, the FAA managers can still talk tough about maintaining standards, but they do not dare suggest that the market has created imbalances and that through re-regulation or more clever mechanisms the hubs may someday have to be abolished and the traffic dispersed. They cannot even state the obvious, that air traffic remains a classic example of the legitimate need for public control.

Self-disdain is of course not the FAA's official policy. The senior managers of air traffic control run 75 percent of the agency's $10 billion budget and direct a force of 20,000 employees. They are strong operators, intelligent, energetic, and decisive, but their work is also heavily saddled with bureaucratic procedure the yearly uncertainty of congressional appropriations and the endless consultations which slow or kill their initiatives. But you need only to listen beyond their words to hear the themes of regret.

The ambivalence at headquarters only reinforces a sense among the controllers, incident by incident, that their managers do not stand up for them but instead, for example, side with the airlines in the persistent and irritating disputes over delays. These disputes have become systematic because to a degree unimagined even by active pilots the FAA has surrendered to free enterprise, allowing the airlines to penetrate every level of air traffic control. Beyond taking a hand in the planning and architecture of the system, the airlines now employ full-time representatives at all the major facilities to question the smallest operational details—a certain flight forced to hold, a certain runway selected because of weather, priority given to one airplane or denied another, a routing or even an altitude assigned. For the airlines big money is involved. But among the controllers the feeling of abandonment is so strong in certain radar rooms that some controllers would be willing to take the entire structure down. The managers know it and in turn feel betrayed by the controllers.

What makes this fight peculiar is the coding which allows it to be waged invisibly. Practically everything about air traffic control—whether it emanates from the controllers, their managers, or the airlines—now has a private as well as a public meaning. For instance, a proposed new arrangement called "free flight" would give pilots more freedom to pick their own routes and more cockpit technology to do it safely, with less guidance from controllers. "Free flight" may mean "smart technology" and "progressive thinking" to outsiders—and it probably *would* increase the capacity of the sky—but it means something quite different to hard-pressed controllers. To them, it is a policy so obviously irrelevant to the bottlenecks on final approach, which greater pilot freedom can only make harder to manage, that it must be interpreted as a coded taunt about the value of controllers and a mean-spirited (if empty) threat about their future. Even when new policies make sense— like the recent systemwide elimination of obsolete flight restrictions, or the reintroduction of inflight holding pools as a way of deriving maximum efficiency from the final approaches—they are interpreted as personal assaults on the working men and women. The controllers fight back through alarmist "equipment failure" articles in the press and through careful cultivation of the safety myth—a tactic especially galling to the managers because of their own lack of credibility with reporters.

The managers like to reassure themselves that many controllers have not joined the union and that at certain Sunbelt facilities nonunion controllers still constitute more than half of the work force. But that hardly means that those controllers have taken their side. The angry Californian who wrote to me had feelings against the union nearly as strong as those against the FAA headquarters. As

I sat beside him one evening at his radar screen, he said, "We made a big mistake when we let in the AFL-CIO. Look at these guys around you, look at their attitude, look how they're dressed. Where's their professionalism? A 'safety issue' for them is a tripping hazard on the stairs. The problem is, *labor* unions represent *laborers.*"

He glumly watched the airplanes moving across his screen. "But you want to know the real problem? Go outside and look how empty the parking lot is after 5:00. Do you remember how full it was this afternoon? What were all those people *doing* today? They can prove in triplicate that the system works. So what? I've gotten so I'm just running out my time. Give me a year and I'll be retired in Florida. I never thought I'd say it, but I'll wish the union well."

When I asked another nonunion controller, at the Fort Worth Center, about the low rate of union participation in Texas, he said, "It's simple. We can afford to watch and wait. It's the big dog theory. Everybody knows it. How goes the Northeast, so goes the country."

And how goes New York, so goes the Northeast.

Also hotly contested is the use of Flow Control, a command facility with formal responsibility for the hour-by-hour functioning of the national system and the power to intervene. Flow Control originally achieved prominence as a rational response to the 1981 strike, enabling a small team at the FAA headquarters, when necessary, to delay takeoffs across the nation in order to keep the reduced staffs at the busiest destinations from being overwhelmed. It was meant to be a fraternal player, the controllers' friend and adviser. Since then, however, it has turned into something quite the opposite. Based in a futuristic radar room near Dulles Airport, it has become a master center with electronic vision that sees every airplane in the system and the authority to question and, in some circumstances, to countermand decisions made by individual controllers. Though it still initiates the departure holds which frustrate pilots and passengers, and though inevitably it miscalculates, causing needless delays, it now sees its mission largely in opposition to the individual control facilities—to keep as many airplanes in the air as possible and maintain pressure on the final approaches. The problem is not simply that controllers and Flow Control often now work at cross purposes; there is also the matter of symbolism. Flow Control has inserted teams into all the regional facilities—specialists who dress better than controllers and work under more relaxed conditions, sometimes from raised islands at the center of the control room floors. Those who say that Flow is just another bureaucratic empire have vastly underestimated it: Whatever its impact on air traffic, it is also Headquarters' greatest hope, free flight's natural companion, a Big Brother with the ability to identify recalcitrant controllers and the authority to intervene and fight back against them. The controllers' union would like nothing more than to break into Flow Control. So far it has been unable to. Now the angriest controllers accuse the union itself of selling out. It is a dangerous sentiment. A similar escalation preceded the ill-considered strike of 1981, but that experience is well remembered, and no one expects the controllers to make such a mistake again. One reason is that the FAA itself provides them with rules and procedures that, if strictly followed, can snarl traffic nearly as effectively as a strike. But such a rule-book slowdown seems heavy-handed, since possibilities abound for more subtle dissent. Renegade job actions in particular can be as spontaneous and creative as a controller's best work, and where the air space is already crowded, they require just a delicate lack of cooperation to produce big results.

With such renegade actions, which have already begun, individual controllers quietly gum up the works. One man described the technique to me this way: "Slow down, speed up, slow down. Now turn right, turn left, stay up, go down." With one airplane you can create a ripple that will last for hours. You can also require unusually large in-trail spacing, or you can simply put airplanes into holding patterns. The details hardly matter, but what they add up to is sabotage.

The pilots involved may not be aware of the reasons for their handling, but increasingly they have begun to question their clearances and to express dissatisfaction on the frequency. Civility is slowly disappearing. But from the controllers' point of view, the beauty of renegade job actions is that they can occur naturally and without premeditation in the political climate of the control rooms, and they are easily deniable, or defensible in the name of safety. The delays they cause are difficult to distinguish from other, ordinary delays. Flow Control can eventually figure out what is happening, and may try to intervene, but usually does so too late. Airline passengers are affected, of course, but that is beside the point.

Once again, the argument is in code. Renegade slow-downs deliver a clear threat within the agency, yet a threat so technical that it remains invisible to the outside world. The public has been frightened into submission. Neither the union nor the FAA will admit that an invisible war has broken out. Air traffic keeps growing, and everyone fears a loss of control.

SEVEN

Valujet 592

ON A MUGGY MAY afternoon in 1996, an emergency dispatcher in southern Florida got a call from a man on a cellular phone. The caller said, "Yes. I am fishing at Everglades Holiday Park, and a large jet aircraft has just crashed out here. Large. Like airliner size."

The dispatcher said, "Wait a minute. Everglades Park?"

"Everglades Holiday Park along canal L-67. You need to get your choppers in the air. I'm a pilot. I have a GPS. I'll give you coordinates."

"Okay sir. What kind of plane did you say? Is it a large plane?"

"A large aircraft similar to a 727 or a umm . . . I can't think of it."

This lapse was unimportant. The caller was a born accident observer—a computer engineer and private pilot with a pride in his technical competence and a passion for detail. His name was Walton Little. When he first saw the airplane it was banked steeply to the right and flying low, just above the swamp. Later he filed an official report in which he wrote:

> There was no smoke, no strange engine noise, no debris in the air, no dangling materials or control surfaces, no apparent deformation of the airframe, and no areas that appeared to have missing panels or surfaces. . . . Sunlight was shining on the aircraft, and some surfaces were more reflective than others. I saw a difference in reflection of the wing skin in the area where I would expect the ailerons to be, as though they were not in neutral. In particular, the lower (outboard) portion of the right wing appeared less reflective as though the aileron was deflected upward.

A couple of nearby fishermen instinctively ducked into their boat for cover, but not Walton Little, who stood on his deck facing "about 115 degrees," and watched the airplane hit the water. The shock wave passed through his body: "I was in disbelief that the crash had occurred. I stood there for just a moment to consider that it really did happen. I was already thinking that I needed to get my cellular phone out of the storage compartment and call 911, but I wanted to assure myself of what I was doing because it is against the law to make false calls to 911."

He called within a minute. After reading off his latitude

and longitude to the dispatcher, he said, "I'm in a bass boat on the canal. I thought it was an aircraft from an air show or something, and—"

The dispatcher interrupted. "What did you . . . Did you see flames and stuff come up, sir?"

"I heard the impact and I saw dirt and mud fly in the air. The plane was sideways before it went out of my sight on the horizon about a mile from me."

"Yes sir. Okay. You said it looked like a 727 that went down?"

"Uh, it's that type aircraft. It has twin engines in the rear. It is larger than an executive jet, like a Learjet."

"Yes sir."

"It's much bigger than that. I won't tell you it's a 727, but it's that type aircraft. No engines on the wing, two engines in the rear. I do not see any smoke, but I saw a tremendous cloud of mud and dirt go into the sky when it hit."

"Okay sir."

"It was white with blue trim."

"White with blue trim, sir?"

"It will not be in one piece."

Walton Little was right. The airplane was a twin-engine DC-9 painted the colors of Valujet, an aggressive young discount airline based in Atlanta. When it hit the Everglades, it was banked vertically to the right and pointed nearly straight down. The airplane did not sink mysteriously into the swamp, as reports later suggested, but shattered against it with the full furious force of a fast dive.

By the time Walton Little felt the shock wave, everyone aboard was dead—the 2 pilots, 3 flight attendants, and 105 passengers. Their remains lay smothered within a shallow, watery crater and the liquid mud and grass that surrounded it. All that marked the surface was a fractured engine, a few dead fish, some jet fuel, and a scattering of personal papers, clothes, and twisted aluminum pieces—the stuff of tragedy. During those first few days some officials worried aloud about the accident's effect on nature, but the swamp was not so fragile as that and quickly resumed its usual life. The families of those who died have proved less resilient.

For the rest of us, though, the accident should be finished business. The official investigation ran its complete course, a "cause" was found, contributing factors were acknowledged, and the Federal Aviation Administration wrote new regulations. Editorialists expressed their outrage, and individuals were held responsible. After a long suspension, Valujet returned to flight with a renewed commitment to safety. Other airlines promised to be more careful, too. And even the FAA went through a housecleaning. By conventional standards, therefore, the reaction to the tragedy was admirable. And yes, we know anyway that flying is safe, that we are a winged species now, that the sky is ours for the taking. Certainly my own experience is that passengers do not need to cower around the exit rows, or carry emergency "smoke hoods," or avoid certain airlines and airplanes, or fear bad weather, or worry about some impending collapse of airline safety. Those are assertions made by aviation illiterates—the overly cautious people who can always gain an audience and who would smother us in their fear of violent death. The public, now a flying public, has the sense in the long run to ignore them. Nonetheless, the Valujet accident continues years later to raise a series of troubling questions—no longer about what happened but about why it happened and what is to keep similar accidents from happening again. As these questions lead into the complicated and human core of flight safety, they become increasingly difficult to answer.

Consider for simplicity that there are only three kinds of airplane accidents. The most common ones you might call "procedural." They are those old-fashioned accidents which result from single obvious mistakes, which can be immediately understood in simple terms, and which lead to simple resolutions. For pilots—do not fly into violent thunderstorms, or take off with ice on your wings, or descend prematurely, or let fear or boredom gain the upper hand. Do not make the mistake of trusting your sense of balance, or as Captain Kukar did on Air India, of feeling too at home in the sky. Mechanics, ramp agents, and air traffic controllers must observe equally simple rules. As practitioners, we have together learned many such painful lessons.

The second sort of accident could be called "engineered." It consists of those surprising material failures which should have been predicted by designers or discovered by test pilots but were not. Such failures at first defy understanding, but ultimately they submit to examination and result in tangible solutions. The American Eagle ATR turboprop dives into a frozen field in Roselawn, Indiana, because its deicing boots did not protect its wings from freezing rain—and as a result, new boots are designed and the entire testing process undergoes review. The USAir Boeing 737 crashes near Pittsburgh because of a rare hardover rudder movement—and as a result a redesigned rudder control mechanism is installed on the whole fleet. The TWA Boeing 747 blows apart off New York because (whatever the source of ignition) the empty center tank contained an explosive mixture of fuel and air—and as a result explosive mixtures might in the future be avoided. Such tragic failures may seem all too familiar, but in fact they are rare, and they will grow rarer still as aeronautical engineering improves. You can regret the lives lost, and deplore the slowness with which officials respond, but in the long run there is reason to be optimistic. Our science will prevail.

But the Valujet accident is different. It represents the third and most elusive kind of disaster, a type of "system accident" which lies beyond the reach of conventional solution and which a small group of thinkers inspired by Yale sociologist Charles Perrow has been exploring elsewhere—in power generation, chemical manufacturing, nuclear weapons control, and space flight. Perrow has coined the more loaded term "normal accident" for such disasters because he believes they are normal for our time. His point is that these accidents are science's illegitimate children, bastards born of the confusion that lies within the complex organizations with which we manage our dangerous technologies. Perrow does not know much about airline flying—and what he says about it he often gets wrong—but his thinking applies to it nonetheless. In this case, the organization includes not only Valujet, the archetype of new-style airlines, but also the contractors who serve it, the government agencies that despite economic deregulation are expected to oversee it, and even the press and Congress, who also play important roles. Taken as a whole, the airline system is complex indeed.

It is also competitive, and if one of its purposes is to make money, the other is to move the public through thin air cheaply and at high speed. Safety is never first, nor can it be, but for obvious reasons it is a necessary companion to the venture. Risk is a companion, too, but on the everyday level of practical compromises and small decisions—the building blocks of this ambitious enterprise—the view of risk is usually obscured. The people involved do not consciously trade safety for money or convenience, but inevitably they do make a lot of bad little choices. They get away with those choices because, as Charles Perrow mentioned to me, Murphy's Law is wrong—what *can* go wrong usually goes *right*. But then one day, a few of the bad little choices combine, and circumstances take an airplane down. Who then really is to blame?

We can find fault among those directly involved—and we probably need to. But if our purpose is to attack the roots of such an accident, we may find them so entwined with the system that they are impossible to extract without bringing the whole structure down. The study of system accidents acts either to radicalize people or to force them to speak frankly. It requires most of us to admit that we do put a price on human life, and that the price, though incalculable, is probably not very high. In the case of Valujet it faces us with the possibility that we have come to depend on flight, that nothing we are willing to do can stop the occasional sacrifice, and that therefore we are all complicitous. Beyond such questions of blame, it requires us to consider the possibility that our solutions, by adding to the complexity and obscurity of the airline business, may actually increase the risk of accidents. System accident thinking does not demand that we accept our fate without a struggle, but it serves as an important caution.

THE DISTINCTION BETWEEN the three types of accidents—procedural, engineered, and system—is of course not absolute. Most accidents have a bit of all three to them. And even in the most extreme cases of system failure, the post-crash investigation has to work its way forward conventionally, usefully identifying those problems which can be fixed, before the remaining questions begin to force a still deeper examination. That was certainly the way with Valujet Flight 592.

It was headed from Miami to Atlanta, flown by Captain Candalyn Kubeck, age thirty-five, and her copilot Richard Hazen, age fifty-two. They represented the new generation of pilots, experienced not only in the cockpit but in the rough-and-tumble of the deregulated airline industry, where each had held a slew of low-paid flying jobs before settling on Valujet. It was no shock to them that Valujet was a nonunion operation or that it required them to pay for their own training. With 9,000 flight hours, over 2,000 in the DC-9, Candalyn Kubeck now earned what the free market said she was worth, about $40,000 a year, plus bonuses; her copilot Richard Hazen, ex-Air Force and with similar experience, earned about half as much. Valujet executives had convinced themselves that the low pay had a positive effect—that it allowed them to employ "real pilots" who just wanted to fly.

But the pilots didn't think about it that way. They felt bruised and probably a little deflated. Sure they wanted to fly, but they worked for Valujet for lack of choice. And they were not the only ones; the flight attendants, ramp agents, and mechanics made a lot less than they would have for a more traditional airline. So much work was farmed out to temporary employees and independent contractors that Valujet was sometimes called a "virtual airline." But why not? FAA regulators had begun to worry that the company was moving too fast and not keeping up on the paperwork, but there was no evidence that the people involved were as individuals inadequate. Many of the pilots were refugees from the labor wars at the old Eastern Airlines, and they were generally as competent and experienced as their higher-paid friends at United, American, and Delta. Valujet was helping the entire industry understand just how far the cost-cutting could be pushed. Its flights were cheap and full, and its stock was strong on Wall Street.

But six minutes out of Miami, while climbing north-west through 11,000 feet, the copilot Richard Hazen radioed, "Ah, 592 needs an immediate return to Miami."

In the deliberate calm of pilot-talk, this was strong language. The time was thirty-two seconds after 2:10 in the afternoon, and the sun was shining. Something had gone wrong with the airplane.

The radar controller at Miami Departure answered immediately. Using Valujet's radio name "Critter" (for the company's cartoonish tail-logo—a smiling airplane) he gave the flight a clearance to turn initially toward the west, away from Miami and conflicting traffic flows, and to begin a descent to the airport. "Critter 592, ah roger, turn left heading two-seven-zero, descend and maintain seven thousand."

Hazen said, "Two-seven-zero, seven thousand, Critter 592."

The controller was Jesse Fisher, age thirty-six, a seven-year veteran, who had twice handled the successful returns of airliners that had lost cabin pressurization. He had worked the night before and had gone home, fed his cat, and slept well. He felt alert and rested. He said, "What kind of problem are you having?"

Hazen said, "Ah, smoke in the cockpit. Smoke in the cabin." His tone was urgent.

Fisher kept his own tone flat. He said, "Roger." Over his shoulder he called, "I need a supervisor here!"

The supervisor plugged in beside him. Flight 592 tracked across Fisher's radar screen, dragging its data tag, which included the automatic readout of the airplane's altitude. Fisher noticed that the pilots had not yet started to turn and descend, and this surprised him. He gave them another heading, farther to the left, and cleared them down to 5,000 feet.

Aboard the airplane, Hazen acknowledged the new heading but misheard the altitude assignment. It didn't matter. Flight 592 was burning, and the situation in the cockpit was rapidly getting out of hand. One minute into the emergency, the pilots were still tracking away from Miami and had not begun their return.

Hazen said, "Critter 592, we need the, ah, closest airport available."

The transmission was garbled or blocked, or Fisher was distracted by competing voices within the radar room. For whatever reason, he did not hear Hazen's request. When investigators later asked him if in retrospect he would have done anything differently, he admitted that he kept asking himself the same question. Even without hearing Hazen's request, he might have suggested some slightly closer airport. But from the airplane's position only twenty-five miles to the northwest of the big airport, Miami International still seemed like the best choice because of the emergency equipment there. In any case "Miami" was the request he *had* heard, and he had intended to deliver it.

To Hazen he said, "Critter 592, they're gonna be standing, standing by for you." He meant the crash crews at Miami. "You can plan Runway 12. When able, direct to Dolphin now."

Hazen said, ". . . need radar vectors." His transmission was garbled by loud background noises. Fisher thought he sounded "shaky."

Fisher answered, "Critter 592, turn left heading one-four-zero."

Hazen said, "One-four-zero." It was his last coherent response.

The flight had only now begun to move through a gradual left turn. Fisher watched the target on his screen as it tracked through the heading changes: The turn tightened, then slowed again. With each sweep of the radar beam, the altitude readouts showed a gradual descent—8,800, 8,500, 8,100. Two minutes into the crisis, Fisher said, "Critter 592, keep the turn around, heading one-two-zero."

Flight 592 may have tried to respond—someone keyed a microphone and transmitted a "carrier" only, without voice.

Fisher said, "Critter 592, contact Miami Approach on—correction, no, you just keep on my frequency."

Two and a half minutes had gone by. It was 2:13 in the afternoon. The airplane was passing through 7,500 feet when suddenly it tightened the left turn and entered a steep dive. Fisher's radar showed the turn and an altitude readout of XXX—code for such a rapid altitude change that the computer could not keep up. Investigators later calculated that the airplane rolled to a sixty-degree left bank and dived 6,400 feet in thirty-two seconds. During that loss of control, Fisher radioed mechanically, "Critter 592, you can, uh, turn left, heading one-zero-zero, and join the Runway 12 localizer at Miami." He also radioed, "Critter 592, descend and maintain three-thousand."

Then the incredible happened. The airplane rolled wings-level again and pulled sharply out of its spiral dive.

Despite what McDonnell-Douglas later claimed about the amazing stability of the DC-9, the airplane would not have done this on its own. It is remotely possible that the autopilot kicked in, that having been disabled by shorting wires, it temporarily re-engaged itself, but it seems more likely from the vigor of the recovery that one of the pilots, having been incapacitated by smoke or defeated by melting control-cables, somehow momentarily regained control. Fisher watched the radar target straighten toward the southeast and again read out a nearly level altitude—however of now merely a thousand feet. The airplane's speed was nearly 500 miles an hour.

The frequency crackled with another unintelligible transmission. Shocked into the realization that the airplane would be unable to make Miami, Fisher said, "Critter 592, Opa Locka Airport's about twelve o'clock at fifteen miles."

Walton Little, in his bass boat, spotted the airplane then, as it rolled steeply to the right. The radar, too, noticed that last quick turn toward the south, just before the final noseover. On the next sweep of the radar, the flight's data block went into "coast" on Fisher's screen, indicating that radar contact had been lost. The supervisor marked the spot electronically, and launched rescue procedures.

Fisher continued to work the other airplanes in his sector. Five minutes after the impact, another low-paid pilot, this one for American Eagle, radioed, "Ah, how did Critter make out?" Fisher did not answer.

* * *

IT WAS KNOWN from the start that fire took the airplane down. The federal investigation began within hours, with the arrival that evening of a National Transportation Safety Board team from Washington. The investigators set up shop in an airport hotel, which they began to refer to without embarrassment as the "command center." The English is important. Similar forms of linguistic stiffness, specifically of engineer-speak, ultimately proved to have been involved in the downing of Flight 592—and this was a factor that the NTSB investigators, because of their own verbal awkwardness, were unable quite to recognize.

It is not reasonable to blame them for this, though. The NTSB is a technical agency, staffed by technicians, and though it makes much of its independence, it occupies a central position in the stilted world of aviation. Its job is to examine important accidents and to issue nonbinding safety recommendations—opinions, really—to industry and government. Because the investigators have no regulatory authority and must rely on persuasion to influence the turn of events, it may even be necessary for them to use impressive, official-sounding language. Even among its opponents, who often feel that its recommendations are impractical, the NTSB has a reputation as a branch of government done right. It is technically competent, and in a world built on compromise, it manages to play the old-fashioned unambiguous role of the public's defender.

The press has a classically symbiotic relationship with the NTSB, relying on the investigators for information while at the same time providing them with their only effective voice. Nonetheless, in times of crisis immediately after an accident, a tension exists between the two. Working under pressure to get the story out, reporters resent the caution of the investigators and their reluctance to speculate off the record. Working under pressure to get the story right, investigators for their part resent the reporters' incessant demands during the difficult first days of an accident probe—the recovery of human remains and airplane parts. By the time I got to Miami, nineteen hours after Flight 592 hit the swamp, the two camps were passing each other warily in the hotel lobby.

Twenty miles to the west, deep in the Everglades, the recovery operation was already under way. The NTSB had set up a staging area—a "forward ops base," one official called it—beside the Tamiami Trail, a two-lane highway that traverses the watery grasslands of southern Florida. Within two days this staging area blossomed into a chaotic encampment of excited officials—local, state, and federal—with their tents and air-conditioned trailers, their helicopters, their cars and flashing lights. I quit counting the agencies. The NTSB had politely excluded most of them from the actual accident site, which lay seven miles to the north, along a narrow levee road.

The press was excluded even from the staging area but was provided with two news conferences a day, during which the investigators warily doled out tidbits of information. One NTSB official said to me, "We've got to feed them or we'll lose control." But the reporters were well behaved and if anything a bit overcivilized. Beside the staging area they settled in to their own little town of television trucks, tents, and lawn chairs. For camera work the location gave them good Everglade backdrops and shots of alligators swimming by; the viewing public could not have guessed that they stood so far from the action. They acted cynical and impatient, but in truth this was not a bad assignment; at its peak their little town boasted pay phones and pizza delivery.

Maybe it was because of my obvious lack of deadlines that the investigators made an exception in my case. They slipped me into the front seat of a Florida Game helicopter whose pilot, in a fraternal gesture, invited me to take the controls for the run out to the crash site. From the staging area, we skimmed north across the swamped grasslands, loosely following the levee road, until swinging wide to circle over the impact zone—a new pond defined by a ring of turned mud and surrounded by a larger area of grass and water and accident debris. Searchers in white protective suits waded line-abreast through the muck, piling pieces of people and airplane into flat-bottomed boats. It was hot and unpleasant work performed in a contained little hell, a place which one investigator later described to me as reeking of jet fuel, earth, and rotting flesh—the special smell of an airplane accident. We descended overhead to touch down on the levee, about 300 yards away from the crash site, where an American flag and a few tents and trucks constituted the recovery base.

The mood there was quiet and purposeful, with no sign among the workers of the emotional trauma that officials had been worriedly predicting since the operation began. The workers on break sat in the shade of an awning, sipping cold drinks and chatting. They were policemen and firemen—not heroes, but straightforward guys accustomed to confronting death as a matter of fact.

It was of course a somber place to be. Human remains lay bagged in a refrigerated truck for later transport to the morgue. A decontamination crew washed down torn and twisted pieces of airplane, none longer than a few feet. Investigators tagged the most promising wreckage to be trucked immediately to a hangar at an outlying Miami airport, where specialists could study it. Farther down the levee I came upon a soiled photograph of a young woman with a small-town face and a head of teased hair. A white-suited crew arrived on an airboat and clambered up the embankment to be washed down. Another crew set off. A boatload of muddy wreckage arrived. The next day, the families of the dead came out from Miami on buses, and laid flowers and cried. After they left, pieces of the airplane kept arriving for nearly another month.

Much was made of this recovery, which—prior to the offshore retrieval of TWA's Flight 800—the NTSB called the most challenging in its history. The swamp did make the search slow and difficult, and the violence of the impact meant that meticulous work was required during the reconstruction of the critical forward cargo hold. However, in truth the Herculean physical part of the investigation served merely to confirm what a simple look at a shipping ticket had already shown—that Valujet Flight 592 burned and crashed not because the airplane failed but because the airline did.

For me the most impressive aspect of the investigation was the speed with which it worked through the false pursuit of an electrical fire—an explanation supported by my own experiences in flight, and made all the more plausible here because the Valujet DC-9 was old and had experienced a variety of electrical failures earlier the same day, including a tripped circuit breaker (for a redundant pump) that had resisted the attentions of a mechanic in Atlanta and then mysteriously had fixed itself. I was impressed also by the instincts of the reporters, who for all their technical ignorance seized upon the news that Flight 592 had been loaded with a potentially dangerous cargo of chemical oxygen generators—scores of little firebombs which could have caused this accident, and indeed did.

Flight 592 crashed on a Saturday afternoon. By Sunday the recovery teams were pulling up scorched and soot-stained pieces. On Monday a searcher happened to step on the flight data recorder, one of the "black boxes" meant to help with accident investigations. The NTSB took the recorder to its Washington laboratory and found there that six minutes after Flight 592's takeoff there had been a blip in the flight data consistent with a momentary rise in air pressure. Immediately afterward the recorder began to fail intermittently, apparently because of electrical power interruptions. On Tuesday night at the hotel press conference, Robert Francis, the vice-chairman of the NTSB and the senior official on the scene, announced in a deliberate monotone, "There could have been an explosion." A hazardous materials team would be joining the investigation. The investigation was focusing on the airplane's forward cargo hold, which was located just below and behind the cockpit and was unequipped with fire detection or extinguishing systems. Routine paperwork indicated that the Miami ground crew had loaded it with homeward-bound Valujet "company material," a witch's brew of three mounted tires and five cardboard boxes of old oxygen generators.

OXYGEN GENERATORS are safety devices. They are small steel canisters mounted in airplane ceilings and seatbacks and linked to the flimsy oxygen masks that dangle in front of the passengers when a cabin loses pressurization. To activate an oxygen flow, the passenger pulls a lanyard, which slides a retaining pin from a spring-loaded hammer, which falls on a minute explosive charge, which in turn sparks a chemical reaction that liberates the oxygen within the sodium chlorate core. This reaction produces heat, which may cause the surface temperature of the canister to rise to 500 degrees Fahrenheit when it is mounted correctly in a ventilated bracket and much higher if the canister is sealed into a box with other canisters, which may themselves be heating up. If the materials surrounding the canister catch fire, the presence of pure oxygen will cause them to burn furiously. If those materials are rubber tires, they will provide a particularly rich source of fuel. Was there an explosion? Perhaps. In any event, Flight 592 was blow-torched into the ground.

It is ironic that the airplane's own emergency oxygen system was different—a set of simple oxygen tanks, similar to those used in hospitals, that grow *colder* during use. The oxygen generators in Flight 592's forward cargo hold came from three MD-80s, a more modern kind of twin-jet, which Valujet had recently purchased and was having refurbished at a hangar across the airport in Miami, As was its practice for most of its maintenance, Valujet had hired an outside company to do the job, in this case a large firm called Sabretech, owned by Sabreliner of St. Louis and licensed by the FAA to perform the often critical work. Sabretech, in turn, had hired other companies to supply contract mechanics on an as-needed basis. It later turned out that three-fourths of the people on the Valujet project were just such temporary outsiders. Many of them held second temporary jobs as well. After the accident, the vulnerability of American wage workers could be seen in their testimonies. They inhabited a world of boss-men and sudden firings, with few protections or guarantees for the future. As the Valujet deadline approached they worked in shifts, day and night, and sometimes through their weekends as well. It was their contribution to our cheap flying.

We will never know everyone at fault in this story. Valujet gave the order to replace the MD-80s' oxygen generators, which had come to the end of their licensed lifetimes. It provided Sabretech with explicit removal procedures and general warnings about the dangers of fire. Over several weeks Sabretech workers extracted the old oxygen generators and tied or cut off their lanyards before stacking them in five cardboard boxes that happened to be lying around the hangar. Apparently they believed that the securing of the lanyards would keep the generators from inadvertently firing off.

What they did *not* do was place the required plastic safety caps over the firing pins—a precaution spelled out on the second line of Valujet's written work order. The problem for Sabretech was that no one had such caps or cared much about finding them. Ultimately, the caps were forgotten or ignored. At the end of the job, in the rush to complete batches of paperwork on all three airplanes, two of the mechanics routinely "pencil-whipped" the problem by fraudulently signing off the safety cap line along with the others certifying that the work had been done. Sabretech inspectors and supervisors signed off on the work, too, apparently without giving the caps much thought.

The timing is not clear. For weeks the five boxes stood on a parts cart beside the airplanes. Eventually a variety of mechanics lugged them over to Sabretech's shipping and receiving department, where they sat on the floor in the area designated for Valujet property. Several days before the accident, a Sabretech manager told the shipping clerk to clean up the area and get all the boxes off the floor in preparation for an upcoming inspection by Continental Airlines, a potential customer. The boxes were unmarked, and the manager did not ask what was in them.

The shipping clerk then did what shipping clerks do and

prepared to send the oxygen generators home to Valujet headquarters in Atlanta. He redistributed them equally between the five boxes, laying the canisters horizontally end to end and packing bubble wrap on top. After sealing the boxes he applied address labels and Valujet company-material stickers and wrote "aircraft parts." As part of the load he included two large main tires, mounted on wheels, and a smaller nose tire. The next day, he asked a co-worker, the receiving clerk, to make out a shipping ticket and to write *Oxygen Canisters—Empty* on it. The receiving clerk wrote *Oxy Canisters,* and then put *Empty* between quotation marks, as if he did not believe it. He also listed the tires.

The cargo stood for another couple of days until May 11, when the company driver had time to deliver them across the airport to Flight 592. There, the Valujet ramp agent accepted the material, though federal regulations forbade him to, even if the generators were empty, because Valujet was not licensed to carry any such officially designated hazardous materials. He discussed the cargo's weight with the copilot, Richard Hazen, who also should have known better. Together they decided to place the load in the forward hold, where Valujet workers laid one of the big main tires flat, placed the nose tire at the center of it, and stacked the five boxes on top of it around the outer edge, in a loose ring. They leaned the other main tire against a bulkhead. It was an unstable arrangement. No one knows exactly what happened then, but it seems likely that the first oxygen generator ignited during the loading, or during the taxiing or on takeoff, as the airplane climbed skyward.

Two weeks later and halfway through the recovery of the scorched and shattered parts, a worker finally found the airplane's cockpit-voice recorder, the second "black box" sought by the investigators. It had recorded normal sounds and conversation up to the same moment—six minutes after takeoff—when the flight data recorder registered a pulse of high pressure. The pulse may have been one of the tires exploding. In the cockpit it sounded like a chirp and a simultaneous beep on the public address system. The captain, Candalyn Kubeck, asked, "What was that?"

Hazen said, "I don't know."

They scanned the airplane's instruments and found sudden indications of electrical failure. It was not the cause but a symptom of the inferno in the hold—the wires and electrical panels were probably melting and burning—but the pilots' first thought was that the airplane was up to its circuit-breaking tricks again. The recording here is garbled. Candalyn Kubeck appears to have asked, "About to lose a bus?" Then more clearly she said, "We've got some electrical problem."

Hazen said, "Yeah. That battery charger's kickin' in. Oooh, we gotta—"

"We're losing everything," Kubeck said. "We need, we need to go back to Miami."

Twenty seconds had passed since the strange chirp in the cockpit. A total electrical failure, though serious, was not in those sunny conditions a life-threatening emergency.

But suddenly now there was incoherent shouting from the passenger cabin, and women and men screaming, "Fire!" The shouting continued for thirteen seconds and subsided.

Kubeck said, "To Miami," and Hazen put in the call to Jesse Fisher, the air traffic controller who the night before had fed his cat and slept well. When Fisher asked, "What kind of problem are you having?" Kubeck answered off radio, "Fire," and Hazen transmitted his urgent, "Smoke in the cockpit, smoke in the cabin."

Investigators now presume that the smoke was black and thick and perhaps poisonous. The recorder picked up the sound of the cockpit door opening and the voice of the chief flight attendant who said, "Okay, we need oxygen, we can't get oxygen back there." Did she mean that people could not breathe, or that the airplane's cabin masks had not dropped, or that they had dropped and were not working? We will never know. But if the smoke was poisonous, the masks might not have helped much anyway, since by design they mix cabin air into the oxygen flow. The pilots were equipped with better isolating-type masks and with goggles but may not have had the time to put them on. Only a minute had passed since the first strange chirp. Now just before it failed, the voice recorder captured the sound of renewed shouting from the cabin. In the cockpit the flight attendant said, "Completely on fire."

The recording was of little use to the NTSB's technical investigation, but because it showed that the passengers had died in agony, it added emotional weight to a political reaction that was already spreading beyond the details of the accident and that had begun to call the entire airline industry into question. The public, it seemed, would not be placated this time by standard reassurances and the discovery of a culprit or two. The press and the NTSB had set aside their on-site antagonism and had joined forces in a natural coalition with Congress. The questioning was motivated not by the immediate fear of unsafe skies (despite the warnings of Mary Schiavo, a federal whistle-blower who stepped forward to claim special insight) but rather by a more nuanced suspicion that competition in the open sky had gone too far and that the FAA, the agency charged with protecting the flying public, had fallen into the hands of industry insiders.

THE FAA'S ADMINISTRATOR then was a one-time airline boss named David Hinson, the sort of glib and self-assured executive who does well in closed circles of like-minded men. Now, however, he would have to address a diverse and skeptical audience. The day after the Valujet accident he had flown to Miami and made the incredible assertion that Valujet was a safe airline—when for 110 people lying dead in a nearby swamp it very obviously was not. He also said, "I would fly on it," as if he believed he had to reassure a nation of children. It was an insulting performance, and it was taken as further evidence of the FAA's isolation and its betrayal of the public's trust.

After a good night's sleep Hinson might have tried to repair the damage. Instead he appeared two days later at a

Senate hearing in Washington sounding like an unrepentant Prussian: "We have a very professional, highly dedicated, organized, and efficient work force that do their job day in and day out. And when we say an airline is safe to fly, it is safe to fly. There is no gray area."

His colleagues must have winced. Aviation safety is nothing but a gray area, and the regulation of it is an indirect process involving negotiation and maneuver. The FAA can affect safety by establishing standards and enforcing them through inspections and paperwork, but it cannot throw the switches in the cockpits or turn the wrenches in the hangars, or in this case supervise the disposal of old oxygen generators. Safety is ultimately in the hands of the operators, the pilots and mechanics and their managers, because it involves a blizzard of small judgments. Hinson might have admitted this, but instead, inexplicably, he chose to link the FAA's reputation to that of Valujet. This placed the agency in an impossible position. It would now inevitably be found to blame.

Within days evidence emerged that certain inspectors at the FAA had been worried about Valujet for years and had included their concerns in their reports. Their consensus was that the airline was expanding too fast (from two to fifty-two airplanes over two and a half years) and that it had neither the procedures nor the people in place to maintain standards of safety. The FAA tried to keep pace, but because of its other commitments—including countering the threat of terrorism—it could assign a crew of only three furiously overloaded inspectors to the entire airline. At the time of the accident they had run 1,471 routine checks on Valujet operations, and 2 additional eleven-day inspections in both 1994 and 1995. Despite the burden it placed on the individual inspectors, this level of scrutiny was, at least on paper, about normal for an airline of this size. But by early 1996, concern had grown within the FAA about the airline's disproportionate number of infractions and its string of small bang-ups. The agency began to move more aggressively. An aircraft maintenance group found such serious problems in both the FAA's field-level surveillance and the airline's operations that it wrote an internal report recommending that Valujet be "recertified" immediately—meaning that it be grounded and started all over again. The report was sent to Washington, where for unexplained reasons it lay buried until after the accident. Meanwhile, on February 22, 1996, headquarters launched a 120-day "special emphasis" inspection, which after the first week issued a preliminary report suggesting a wide range of problems. The special emphasis inspection was ongoing when, on May 11, Flight 592 went down.

As this record of official concern emerged, the questions changed from why Hinson had insisted on calling Valujet "safe" after the accident to why he had not shut down the airline *before* the accident. Trapped by his earlier simplistic formulations, he could provide no convincing answer. The press and Congress jeered. The FAA now launched an exhaustive thirty-day review of Valujet, the most concentrated airline inspection in U.S. aviation history, assigning sixty inspectors to perform in one month the equivalent of four years' work. Lewis Jordan, the founder and president of Valujet, complained that Hinson was playing to the mob and conducting a witch hunt that no airline could withstand. Jordan had been trying shamelessly to shift the blame for the deaths onto his own cut-rate contractor, Sabretech, and he received little sympathy now. But he was right about the witch hunt. Even when Valujet did things right under the pressure of the inspection, the results were compared to earlier statistics to demonstrate that when the inspectors were not present Valujet normally did things wrong. Five weeks after the accident, it was a surprise to no one when Valujet was indefinitely grounded.

Here now was the proof that the FAA had earlier neglected its duties. The agency's chief regulator, Anthony Broderick, was the first to lose his job. Broderick was an expert technocrat, disliked by safety crusaders because of his cautious approach to regulation and respected by aviation insiders for the same reason. Hinson pushed him out in front, knowing that he was a man of integrity and would accept responsibility for the FAA's poor performance. But if Hinson thought that he himself could escape with this sacrifice, he was wrong. Broderick's airline friends now joined the critics in disgust, and the jeering grew so loud that Hinson was forced from office.

In that sense the system worked. One year after the accident it was possible to conclude that the tragedy had perhaps had some positive consequences—primarily because the NTSB had done an even better job than usual, not only of pinpointing the source and history of the fire but of recognizing some of its larger implications. With a well-timed series of press feedings and public hearings, the accident team had kept the difficult organizational issues alive and had managed to stretch the soul-searching through the end of the year and beyond. By shaking up the FAA, the team had reminded the agency of its original responsibilities—prodding it perhaps into a renewed commitment to inspections and a resolution to impose greater responsibility on the airlines for their actions, including the performance of outside shops.

For the airlines, the investigation served as a necessary reminder of the possible consequences of cost cutting and complacency. Among airline executives smart enough to notice, it may also have served as a warning about the public's growing distrust of their motivations and about widespread anger with the whole business—anger that may have as much to do with the way passengers are handled as with their fears of dying. However you wanted to read it, the Valujet turmoil marked the limits of the public's tolerance. The airlines were cowed, and they submitted eagerly to the banning of oxygen generators as cargo on passenger flights. Having lost their friend Broderick, they then rushed ahead of the FAA with a $400 million promise (not yet fulfilled) to install fire detectors and extinguishers in all cargo holds. As it had before, the discussion of hidden cargo hazards ran up against the practical difficulties of inspection. Nonetheless, after the accident the ground crews could be counted on for a while to watch what they loaded into airplanes and what they took out and threw away.

And the guilty companies? They were sued, of course, and lost money. After firing the two mechanics who had fraudulently signed the work orders, Sabretech tried to put its house in order. Nonetheless, its customers fled and did not return. The Miami operation dropped from 650 to 135 employees and in January 1997 was forced to close its doors. Soon afterward, as the result of a three-month FAA investigation, Sabretech's new Orlando facility was forced to close as well. Valujet survived its grounding and under intense FAA scrutiny returned to the sky toward the end of 1996, with a reduced and standardized fleet of DC-9s. Because of continuing public worries it changed its name to Airtran, and for a while it was probably the safest airline in the country. What then explains the feeling, particular to this case, that so little has in reality been achieved?

CHARLES PERROW came unintentionally to his theories about "normal accidents" after studying the failings of large organizations. His point is not that some technologies are riskier than others, which is obvious, but that the control and operation of some of the riskiest technologies like nuclear power generation and some chemical manufacturing require organizations so complex that serious failures are virtually guaranteed to occur. Those failures will occasionally combine in unforeseeable ways, and if they induce further failures in an operating environment of tightly interrelated processes, the failures will spin out of control, defeating all interventions. The resulting accidents are inevitable, Perrow observes, because they emerge from the very heart of the ventures. You cannot eliminate one without killing the other.

Perrow's insight has the power of an authentic observation. It tends to impose its logic across pre-existing ideological lines and in unanticipated ways. Perrow himself has run up against it: He is a moralist with an urge to blame elites for the failings of their organizations, and in examining some of the more notorious modern cases he has drawn back from what his own theory coolly suggests— that good and evil were not ultimately at play.

I went to see Perrow one rainy day in New Haven and suggested to him that his observations could be used to excuse the bad decisions of big business. He stood up and began pacing his brick-walled office, exclaiming that this of course was not what he had intended. I pursued the subject. After a while he seemed delighted to claim that I had stumped him.

At sixty-two, Perrow is a burly and disheveled man with a fleshy face and the dust of old rebellions about him. He is affable, excitable, physically restless, strong, and no doubt a bit reckless. I got the impression that his students must enjoy him. As a teacher he is at his best as a generalist, heated and irrepressible, spinning off new ideas, acknowledging his errors, and confidently moving on. He is also a storyteller, and accidents are his passion; even in print he wanders into their unimportant details and loses track of his larger subjects. During our conversation about Valujet he diverged into an irrelevant description of a barge collision and then apologized with a self-deprecating smile, calling himself "an accident maven."

Beneath his affability, however, I saw a seriousness in his eyes and in the unexpected soberings of his facial expressions. I won't link this directly to his professional contemplation of catastrophe, because like most of us Perrow must deal with horror in the abstract; his sudden soberings may be related simply to his intelligence or his age. Nonetheless, I got the impression that he rarely loses sight of the human suffering contained within his musings. When a reporter from the New York *Times* called, fishing for a quote on an accident, Perrow grew angry and hung up on him abruptly, after snapping, "The people I talk to are graduate students. The New York *Times* lacks the sophistication." I thought this was unfair, since the New York *Times* had just proved itself with that phone call. Perrow is precisely the man who can explain why the-news-that's-fit-to-print is so regularly the news of disaster.

In fact it seemed to me, sitting in his office, that Perrow had just hung up on one of his natural allies. His natural opponents are people like me—at least in the general sense. Pilots are safety practitioners, steeped in a can-do attitude toward survival, fluent in the language of collective learning, confident in their own skills, trained to "fly the airplane" to the end. My secret emotion at the Valujet crash site was not compassion or sadness but annoyance with the dead crew. So what if they had a fire, I thought—

they still should not have lost control. If that reaction seems too severe, for an active pilot it is nonetheless probably healthy. As a child of the sky, before I first soloed, I was taken aside by my pilot-father, who rather than talking about the risks that lay ahead simply said, "If you are crossing the street at a crosswalk, and some drunk driver runs you over, then it is your own fault for being there in the first place." And I understood even then that he was right. Pilots have to take their fate firmly into their own hands. Airplanes speak to them through their controls, but they remain inanimate machines and mindlessly unforgiving. I took a job with a great Texas airman named Fritz Kahl, who upon seeing "God Is My Copilot" stenciled below a pilot's window once remarked to me, "Any son of a bitch who needs God to fly beside him oughta stay on the goddamned ground." And he was right, too. Pilots are not paid to wonder.

The basis for such an attitude is the idea that man-made accidents must by definition lie within human control. The strongest proponents of this approach are a group of Berkeley professors—notably the political scientist Todd La Porte—who study "high-reliability organizations," meaning those with good track records at handling apparently risky technologies—aircraft carriers, air traffic control centers, certain power companies. They search for elements which might explain the high levels of safety already achieved and which might be extended to produce perfect safety.

These high-reliability theorists object to being called

"optimistic," which sounds to them like "naïve." They say they accept the inevitability of human error and mechanical failure, and they deny that they use a "closed" organizational model—one that simplistically assumes that civilian organizations might, like military units, be isolated from the confusions of the larger society. Nonetheless, they work with the idea that organizations can be made superior to the sum of their parts, that redundancies count, that decision making and formal responsibilities can be centralized or decentralized according to need, that organizations are rational beings which learn from past mistakes and can tailor themselves to achieve new objectives, and that if the right steps are taken, accidents can be avoided. A zero-accident rate, they say, is a theoretical possibility.

Perrow studied at Berkeley and once worked with some of the high-reliability theorists, but his thinking grew up beside theirs, not in reaction to it. It has close but unacknowledged ties to the idea of chaos in the natural world—the disorder discovered by Edward Lorenz that frustrates forecasts and limits practical science. More explicitly, Perrow's accident theory grows from a skeptical view of large organizations as overly rigid, internally divided, and inherently unfocused systems—collectives that resist learning, gloss over failures, suffer from internal conflicts and confusion, and defy rational plans.

This approach was refined in the 1970s by sociologist James March, who wrote about "organized anarchies," and coined the term "garbage can" to characterize their internal functioning—a bewildering mix of solutions looking for problems, inconsistent and ill-defined goals, fluid and uninformed participation in decision making, changes in the outside world, and pure chance as well. Of course, organizations do succeed in producing products, including services like safe airline flying. The garbage can model explains the reasons only for their difficulties, but it does so with a ring of truth among executives long frustrated by their lack of direct control.

Perrow uses the garbage can model to explain why institutional failures are unavoidable, even "normal," and why when organizations are required to handle dangerous technologies safely, they regularly do not. By necessity these are the very organizations that claim, often sincerely, to put safety first. Their routine failures sometimes become Perrow's "normal accidents" and may blossom as they did for the FAA and Valujet into true catastrophes.

Perrow's seminal book, *Normal Accidents: Living with High Risk Technologies* (1984), is a hodgepodge of storytelling and exhortation, weakened by contradiction and factual error, out of which however this new way of thinking has risen. His central device is an organizational scale against which to measure the likelihood of serious "system" accidents. He does not assign a numerical index to the scale but uses a set of general risk indicators. On the low end stand the processes—like those of most manufacturing—that are simple, slow, linear, and visible, and in which the operators experience failures as isolated and containable events. At the other end stand the opaque and tangled processes characterized by a combination of what Perrow calls "interactive complexity" and "close coupling."

By "interactive complexity" he means not simply that there are many elements involved but that those elements are linked to one another in multiple and often unpredictable ways. The failure of one part—whether material, psychological, or organizational—may coincide with the failure of an entirely different part, and this unforeseeable combination will cause the failure of other parts, and so on. If the system is large, the combinations are practically infinite. Such unravelings seem to have an intelligence of their own; they expose hidden connections, neutralize redundancies, bypass "firewalls," and exploit chance circumstances which no engineer could have anticipated. When the operating system is also inherently quick (like a chemical process, an automated response to missile attack, or a jet airliner in flight), the cascading failures will accelerate out of control, confounding the human operators and denying them a chance to jerry-rig a recovery. That lack of slack is Perrow's "close coupling." Then the only difference between an accident and a human tragedy may be a question, as in chemical plants, of which way the wind blows.

I ran across this thinking by chance, a year before the Valujet crash, when I picked up a copy of Scott D. Sagan's book, *The Limits of Safety: Organizations, Accidents, and Nuclear Weapons* (1993). Sagan is a Stanford political scientist, as fastidious and contained a man as Perrow is not. He is a generation younger, the sort of deliberate careerist who moves carefully between posts in academia and the Pentagon. Unlike Perrow, he seems drawn to safety for personal as well as public reasons. Perrow needed such an ally. Sagan is the most persuasive of his interpreters, and with *The Limits of Safety* he has solidified system accident thinking, focusing it more clearly than Perrow was able to. The book starts by opposing high-reliability and normal-accident theories, then tests them against a laboriously researched and previously secret history of failures within U.S. nuclear weapons operations. The test is a transparent artifice, but it serves to define the opposing theories. Sagan's obvious bias does not diminish his work.

Strategic weapons pose an especially difficult problem for system-accident thinking for two reasons: First, there has never been an accidental nuclear detonation, let alone an accidental nuclear war; and second, if a real possibility of such an apocalyptic failure exists, it threatens the very logic of nuclear deterrence—the expectation of rational behavior on which we continue to base our arsenals. Once again the pursuit of system accidents leads to uncomfortable ends. Sagan is not a man to advocate disarmament, and he shies away from it here, observing realistically that nuclear weapons are here to stay. Nonetheless, once he has defined "accidents" as less than nuclear explosions—as false warnings, near launches, and other unanticipated breakdowns in this ultimate "high-reliability" system—Sagan discovers a pattern of such accidents, some of which were contained only by chance. The reader is hardly surprised when Sagan concludes that the accidents were inevitable.

The book interested me not because of the catastrophic potential of such accidents but because of the quirkiness of the circumstances that underlay so many of them. It was a quirkiness which seemed uncomfortably familiar to me. Though it represented possibilities that I as a pilot had categorically rejected, this new perspective required me to face the wild side of my own experience with the sky. I had to admit that some of my friends had died in crazy and unlucky ways, that some flights had gone uncontrollably wrong, and that perhaps not even the pilots were to blame. What is more, I had to admit that no matter how carefully I checked my own airplanes and how deliberately now I flew them, the same could happen to me.

That is where we stand now as a society with Valujet, and it explains our continuing discomfort with the accident. Flight 592 burned because of its cargo of oxygen generators, yes, but more fundamentally because of a tangle of confusions which the next time will take some entirely different form. It is frustrating to fight such a phenomenon. At each succeeding level of inquiry we seize upon the evidence of wrongdoing, only to find after reflection that our outrage has slipped away. Flight's greatest gift is to let us look around, to explore the inner world of sky, but also in the end to bring us back down again, and leave us facing ourselves.

TAKE, FOR EXAMPLE, the case against the two Sabretech mechanics who removed the oxygen canisters from the Valujet MD-80s, ignored the written work orders to install the safety caps, stacked the dangerous canisters improperly in the cardboard boxes, and finished by fraudulently signing off on a job well done. They will probably suffer much of their lives for their negligence, as perhaps they should. But here is what really happened. Nearly 600 people logged work time against the three Valujet airplanes in Sabretech's Miami hangar; of them, 72 workers logged 910 hours across several weeks against the job of replacing the "expired" oxygen generators—those at the end of their approved lives. According to the supplied Valujet work card 0069, the second step of the seven-step removal process was: *If generator has not been expended, install shipping cap on the firing pin.*

This required a gang of hard-pressed mechanics to draw a distinction between canisters that *were* "expired," meaning the ones they were removing, and canisters that were *not* "expended," meaning the same ones, loaded and ready to fire, on which they were now expected to put nonexistent caps. Also involved were canisters which were expired and expended, and others which were not expired but were expended. And then, of course, there was the simpler thing—a set of new replacement canisters, which were both unexpended and unexpired.

If this language seems confusing, do not waste your time trying to sort it out. The Sabretech mechanics certainly did not, nor should they have been expected to. The NTSB later suggested that one problem at Sabretech's Miami facility was the large number of Spanish-speaking immigrants on the work force, but quite obviously the language problem lay on the other side—with Valujet and the narrowly educated English-speaking engineers who wrote work orders and technical manuals as if they were writing to themselves.

Eleven days after the accident, one of the hapless mechanics who had signed off on the work still seemed unclear about basic distinctions between the canisters. An NTSB agent asked him about a batch of old oxygen generators, removed from the MD-80s, that the mechanic had placed in a box.

AGENT: Okay. Where were they?

MECHANIC: On the table.

AGENT: On the table?

MECHANIC: Yes.

AGENT: And there were only how many left to do? (He meant old oxygen generators to be replaced, remaining in the airplane.)

MECHANIC: How many left?

AGENT: Yeah. You said you did how many?

MECHANIC: Was like eight or twelve, something like that.

AGENT: Eight or twelve left?

MECHANIC: The rest were already back in the airplane.

AGENT: The new ones?

MECHANIC: Yes.

AGENT: What about the old ones?

MECHANIC: The old ones?

AGENT: Yeah. Yeah, that's the one we're worried about, the old ones.

MECHANIC: You're worried about the old ones?
AGENT: Yeah.

But that was after the accident. Before the accident, the worry was not about old parts but about new ones—the safe refurbishing of the MD-80s in time to meet the Valujet deadline. The mechanics quickly removed the oxygen canisters from the brackets and wired green tags to most of them. The green tags meant "repairable," which these canisters were not. It is not clear how many of the seventy-two workers were aware that the canisters could not be used again, since the replacement of oxygen generators is a rare operation, though most claimed after the accident to have known at least why the canisters had to be removed. But here, too, there is evidence of confusion. After the accident, two tagged canisters were found still lying in the Sabretech hangar. On one of the tags under "Reason for removal" someone had written, "Out of date." On the other tag someone had written, "Generators have been ~~expired~~ fired."

Yes, a perfect mechanic might have found his way past the Valujet work card, and into the massive MD-80 Maintenance Manual, to chapter 35-22-01, within which line "h" would have instructed him to "store or dispose of oxygen generator." By diligently pursuing these two options, he could eventually have found his way to a different part of the manual and learned that "all serviceable and unserviceable (unexpended) oxygen generators (canisters) are to be stored in an area that ensures each unit is not exposed to high temperatures or possible damage." By pondering the structure of that sentence he might have deduced that "unexpended" canisters are also "unserviceable" canisters, and therefore perhaps should be taken to a safe area and "initiated" according to the procedures provided in section 2.D.

To "initiate" an oxygen generator is, of course, to fire it off, triggering the chemical reaction that produces oxygen and leaves a mildly toxic residue within the canister, which then is classified as a hazardous waste. Section 2.D ends with the admonition that "an expended oxygen generator (canister) contains both barium oxide and asbestos fibers and must be disposed of in accordance with local regulatory compliances and using authorized procedures." No wonder the mechanics stuck the old generators in boxes.

The supervisors and inspectors failed miserably here, though after the accident they proved clever at ducking responsibility. At the least they should have supplied the required safety caps and verified that those caps were being used. If they had—despite all the other errors that were made—Flight 592 would not have burned. For larger reasons, too, their failure is an essential part of this story. It represents not the avarice of profit takers but rather something more insidious, the sort of collective relaxation of technical standards that Boston College sociologist Diane Vaughan has called "the normalization of deviance" and that she believes existed at NASA in the years leading to the 1986 explosion of the space shuttle *Challenger*. The leaking o-ring that caused the catastrophic blow-through of rocket fuel was a well-known design weakness, and it had been the subject of worried memos and conferences up to the eve of the launch. Afterward it was widely claimed that the decision to launch anyway had been made because of political pressure from the top—the agency was drifting, its budget was threatened, and the leadership from the White House down wanted to avoid the embarrassment of an expensive delay. But after an exhaustive exploration of NASA's closed and technical world, Vaughan concluded that the real problems were more cultural than political and that the error had actually come from below. Simply put, NASA had proceeded with the launch despite its o-ring worries largely because it had gotten away with launching the o-ring before. What can go wrong usually goes right—and people just naturally draw the wrong conclusions. In a general way, this is what happened at Sabretech. Some mechanics now claim to have expressed their concerns about the safety caps, but if they did they were not heard. The operation had grown used to taking shortcuts.

But let's be honest. Mechanics who are too careful will never get the job done. Whether in flight or on the ground, the airline system requires the people involved to compromise, to improvise, and sometimes even to gamble. The Sabretech crews went astray—but not far astray—by allowing themselves quite naturally not to worry about discarded parts.

A fire hazard? Sure. The mechanics tied off the lanyards and shoved the canisters a little farther away from the airplanes they were working on. The canisters had warnings about heat on them, but none of the standard hazardous material placards. It probably would not have mattered anyway because the work area was crowded with placards and officially designated hazardous materials, and people had learned not to take them too seriously. Out of curiosity, a few of the mechanics fired off some canisters and listened to the oxygen come out—it went *pssst*. Oh yeah, the things got hot, too. No one even considered the possibility that the canisters might accidentally be shipped. The mechanics did finally carry the five cardboard boxes over to the shipping department, but only because that was where Valujet property was stored—an arrangement that itself made sense.

The shipping clerk was a regular fellow. When he got to work the next morning, he found the boxes without explanation on the floor of the Valujet area. The boxes were innocent-looking, and he left them alone until he was told to tidy up. Sending them to Atlanta seemed like the best way to do that. He had shipped off "company material" before without Valujet's specific approval, and he had heard no complaints. He knew he was dealing now with oxygen canisters but apparently did not understand the difference between oxygen storage tanks and chemical generators designed to fire off. When he prepared the boxes for shipping, he noticed the green "repairable" tags mistakenly placed on the canisters by the mechanics, and he misunderstood them to signify "unserviceable" or "out of service," as he variably said after the accident. He also drew the unpredictable conclusion that the canisters were therefore empty. He asked the receiving clerk to fill out a shipping ticket.

The receiving clerk did as he was instructed, listing the tires and canisters, but he put quotation marks around the word "empty." Later, when asked why, he replied, "No reason. I always put like, when I put my check, I put 'Carlos' in quotations. No reason I put that."

The reason was, it was his habit. On the shipping ticket he also wrote "5 boxes" between quotation marks—a nonsensical use of punctuation which in context now can be taken to mean not that Carlos suspected there were fewer boxes or more but by implication that he too believed the oxygen canisters were empty.

Two days later, over by Flight 592 the Valujet ramp agent who signed for the cargo did not care about such subtleties anyway. Valujet was not authorized to carry hazardous cargoes of any sort, and it seems obvious now that a shipping ticket listing inflated tires and oxygen canisters (whether "empty" or not) should have aroused the ramp agent's suspicions. No one would have complained had he opened the boxes or summarily rejected the load. There was no "hazardous material" paperwork associated with it, but he had been formally trained in the recognition of unmarked hazards. His Valujet Station Operations Manual specifically warned that "cargo may be declared under a general description that may have hazards which are not apparent, that the shipper may not be aware of this. You must be conscious of the fact that these items have caused serious incidents, and in fact, endangered the safety of the aircraft and personnel involved." It also warned:

Your responsibility in recognizing hazardous materials is dependent on your ability to: 1. Be Alert! 2. Take time to ask questions! 3. Look for labels . . . Ramp agents should be alert whenever handling luggage or boxes. Any item that might be considered hazardous should be brought to the attention of your supervisor or pilot, and brought to the immediate attention of Flight Control and, if required, the FAA. REMEMBER: SAFETY OF PASSENGERS AND FELLOW EMPLOYEES DEPENDS ON YOU!

It is possible that the ramp agent was lulled by the company-material labels. Would the Sabretech workers, aviation insiders, ship him a hazardous cargo of his own material without letting him know? His conversation with the copilot, Richard Hazen, about the weight of the load may have lulled him as well. Hazen, too, had been formally trained to spot hazardous materials, and he would have understood better than the ramp agent the dangerous nature of oxygen canisters, but he said nothing. It was a routine moment in a routine day. The morning's pesky electrical problems had perhaps been resolved. The crew was calmly and rationally preparing the airplane for the next flight. As a result, the passengers' last line of defense folded.

WHAT ARE WE TO MAKE of this tangle of circumstance and error? One suspicion is that its causes may lie in the market forces of a deregulated airline industry and that in order to keep such accidents from happening again we might consider the possibility of re-regulation—a return to the old system of limited competition, union work forces, higher salaries, and expensive tickets. There are calls, of course, to do just that. The improvement in safety would come from slowing things down and allowing a few anointed airlines the leisure to discover their mistakes and to act on them. The effects on society, however, would be inflationary and anti-egalitarian—a return to a constricted system that most people could not afford to use. Moreover, aviation history would argue against it. Despite the obvious chaos of the business and the apparent regularity of airline accidents, air travel has become safer under deregulation. Much of that improvement comes from technical advances that would have occurred anyway—those that have resulted in the continued reduction of "procedural" and "engineered" accidents.

The other way to regulate the airline industry is not economic but operational—detailed governmental oversight of all the technical aspects of flight. This is the approach we have taken since the birth of the airlines in the 1920s, and it is what we expect of the FAA today. Strictly applied standards are all the more important in a free market, in which unchecked competition would eventually force the airlines to cut costs to the point of operating unsafely, until accidents forced each in turn out of business. An airline should not overload its airplanes or fly them with worn-out parts, but it also cannot compete effectively against other airlines that do. Day to day, airline executives may resent the intrusion of government, but in their more reflective moments they must also realize that they *need* this regulation in order to survive. The friendship that has grown up between the two sides—between the regulators and the regulated—is an expression of this fact which no amount of self-reform at the FAA can change. When after the Valujet crash David Hinson of the FAA reacted to accusations of cronyism by going to Congress and humbly requesting that the agency's "dual mandate" be eliminated, so that it would no longer be required by law to promote the airlines, he was engaged in a particularly hollow form of political theater.

The critics had real points to make. The FAA had become too worried about the reactions of its friends in the airline industry, and it needed to try harder to enforce the existing regulations. Perhaps it needed even to write some new regulations. And like NASA before, it needed to listen to the opinions and worries of its own lower-level employees. But there are limits to all this, too. The dream of a zero-accident future is about as realistic as the old Valujet promise to put safety first. When at a post-crash press conference in Miami a reporter asked Robert Francis of the NTSB, "Shouldn't the government protect us against this kind of thing?" the honest answer would have been, "It cannot, and never will."

The truth helps because in our frustration with such accidents we are tempted to invent solutions that, by adding to the obscurity and complexity of the system, may aggravate just those characteristics which led to the accidents in the first place. This argument for a theoretical point of *diminishing* safety is a central part of Perrow's thinking, and it seems to be borne out in practice. In his exploration of the North American early warning system, Sagan found that it was failures of safeties and redundancies that gave the most dangerous false indications of missile attack—the kind that could have triggered a response. The radiation accidents at both the Chernobyl and the Three Mile Island power plants were induced by failures in the safety systems. Remember also that the Valujet oxygen generators were safety devices, that they were redundant, and that they were removed from the MD-80s because of regulations limiting their useful lives. This is not an argument against such devices but a reminder that elaboration comes at a price.

Human reactions add to the problem. Administrators can think up impressive chains of command and control and impose complex double-checks and procedures on an operating system, and they can load the structure with redundancies, but there comes a point—in the privacy of a cockpit or a hangar or an office or a house—beyond which people will rebel. These rebellions are commonplace, and they result in unpredictable and apparently arbitrary actions, all the more so because in the modern insecure workplace they remain undeclared. The one thing that always gets done right is the required paperwork.

The paperwork is a necessary and inevitable part of the system, but it, too, introduces dangers. The problem is not just its wastefulness but the deception that it breeds. In the Sabretech hangar the two unfortunate mechanics who signed the lines about the nonexistent safety caps just happened to be the slowest to slip away when the supervisors needed signatures. The other mechanics almost certainly would have signed, too, as did the inspectors. Their good old-fashioned pencil whipping is the most widespread form of Vaughan's "normalization of deviance."

The fraud they committed was a small part of a much larger deception—the creation of fully formed pretend realities that include unworkable chains of command, unlearnable training programs, unreadable manuals, and the fiction of regulations, checks, and controls. Such pretend realities are familiar to all of us. They extend even into the most self-consciously progressive organizations, with their attempts to formalize informality, deregulate the workplace, share profits and responsibilities, respect the integrity and initiative of the individual. The systems work in principle, and usually in practice as well, but the two may have little to do with each other.

No one is to blame for this divergence, and there may be no way to avoid it, but we might now begin to see how the pretend realities lie falsely within our new world like the old-fashioned parks of a formal landscape. We can hide for a while in our fantasies of agreement and control, but ultimately we cannot escape the vernacular terrain—the cockpits and hangars and auto body shops, the lonely lit farmhouses sailing backward through the night—where we continue to struggle through life on the face of a planet.

We have come to a point in history not of an orderly

existence but of something less expected: the possibility of seeing ourselves reflected perfectly in the turbulence and confusion that exists inside the sky. This gives me hope. It means that the sky is not some separate place but a vast new extension of our human earth, and that I as a pilot have perhaps not wasted my time there. Flight's greatest gift is to let us look around, and when we do we discover that the world is larger than we have been told and that our wings have helped to make it so.

ALSO BY WILLIAM LANGEWIESCHE

SAHARA UNVEILED
A Journey Across the Desert

It is as vast as the United States and so arid that most bacteria cannot survive there. William Langewiesche came to the Sahara to see it as its inhabitants do, riding its public transport, braving its natural and human dangers, depending on its sparse sustenance and suspect hospitality. From his journey, which took him across the desert's hyperarid core from Algiers to Dakar, he has crafted a contemporary classic of travel writing.

"Langewiesche makes the desert's exoticism bloom. . . .
The writing has a finely observed, austere beauty."
—*Newsday*

Travel/0-679-75006-1